JOURNEY

OF THE

SON

By Marcus Santi

© 2015

JOURNEY OF THE SON
published by Thrilling Life Publishers
P.O. Box 92522
Southlake, TX 76092
www.thrillinglife.com

Copyright © 2015 by Marcus Santi
ALL RIGHTS RESERVED

Printed in the United States of America
International Standard Book Number: 978-0-9849220-4-8
Cover design by Just Ink Digital Design

Scripture quotations are from:
The Holy Bible, New International Version © 1973, 1984
by International Bible Society, used by permission of
Zondervan Publishing House
No part of this publication may be reproduced, stored in
a retrieval system, or transmitted, in any form or by any
means – electronic, mechanical, photocopying, recording,
or otherwise – without prior written permission of the
author.

Thrilling Life Publishers
Memoir
Helping you Pursue a Thrilling Life – John 10:10
www.thrillinglife.com
www.thrillinglife.com/journeyoftheson

TABLE OF CONTENTS

An open letter from Marcus 5
Chapter 1 - Life is a Race with Hurdles ... 7
    Every Step You Take 18
    You Are Not Alone 25
    It's the Small Things 26
    Heart 30

Chapter 2 - An Olympiad of Time 35
Chapter 3 - Runners To Your Mark 47
    Like Father Like Son 54

Chapter 4 - Vincero Vincero Vincero 59
    No Excuses 68
    I Want to Know What Love Is 73

Chapter 5 - Track is My Sanctuary 79
    Love in Action 81
    Choices 83

Chapter 6 - Burning Questions 87
    Dysfunction invites Co- Dependency 91

Chapter 7 - The Point of the Great Divide 101
The Darkest Hours 104
Rising from the Ashes 110
UP UP and Away 120

Chapter 8 - The Choice: Darth Vader vs Luke Skywalker 131
Healing Begins with Giving 137
A New Beginning 139
The Empire Strikes Back 144
Believe What You Think 149

Chapter 9 - Walls Come Tumbling Down 153
Generational Curses & Track Records 157

Chapter 10 - The Gold Medal 163

Chapter 11 - Guardian Angel 173

The Eulogy 179

Special Thanks 190-191

About the Author 192-193

An Open Letter

You hold in your hand the story of my journey. It is the journey of a son—my father's son, me. We are all on a journey in this life. Some walk a journey that begins easy, idealistic, fairy tale. Others, not so much, instead their journey is filled with pain, betrayal, detours with occasional glimmers of hope. The latter was my journey.

Following is a true story I hope will help those searching for answers in their own journey, offer wake-up bells to those allowing their own pain to harm others, and a challenge for those on an easier journey to step out and help your fellow man on his race to the finish.

Marcus Santi

SUPERMAN

Dad and I running a 5k race when I was a child

Chapter 1

LIFE IS A RACE WITH HURDLES

July 7, 2007:

My phone rings. I look at the phone; it's my father calling me. At this point in time we would speak about twice each month. I had a hard time trusting my father. Everything I would say to him he would use against me at some point. This particular conversation was unusual. He took me down memory lane. He was telling me stories of the past, asking me if I remembered those times. I did remember those times. He ended the conversation by telling me "I love you a lot, son." I thanked him and told him I loved him too. It was hard for me to accept this comment from him. Why? Because for so many years I had been conditioned to look for what was coming. It's like listening to someone who is telling you to look "over there" because they didn't want you to see the right hook they were about to hit you with.

That is how it was with dad. Somewhere inside of me, I knew what he was telling me was his truth. There wasn't a right hook coming; he was not up to anything malevolent – he was telling me honestly that he loved me. 1985 was the last time I remember feeling these words my father had just spoken to me. Sure he said them after 1985 but it was never the same. On this day; 7/7/07 it was just like what I felt when hearing "I love you son" from 1971-1985.

I hung up the phone, dumbfounded and shocked. *What was that?* I told the people I was living with: "It is like someone is going to die. It was a complete conversation." The call is what I called a bookend conversation. It was a completion to our relationship – a relationship that had started off great, experienced its rough stages, and now, by this phone exchange, had been brought back to its beginning. This was the level and type of love I felt from my father for the first 10 years of my life.

July 16, 2007:

Whether I know it definitively or not,

somewhere in my subconscious is a little boy who still believes dad will catch me in his arms if I jump from the top of the proverbial high stairs. I think this is what hit me the hardest as I looked upon the reality of seeing my "Superman" fight for his life.

My father's internal suffering had taken the form of extreme external suffering – what a pill to swallow for those who love my Superman. The abuse from his own father, the emotional wounds he never let go of – wounds he couldn't run from – led him to believe that a bullet to the head would silence his pain. This reality was so stunning that I could not stand as I looked upon my Superman.

I have a dad who hurt so badly that he wanted to end his life. This is a thought and a reality I will live with for the rest of my life.

I feel as though we are again back to where our relationship started when I was a child, but now we had both become adults. I felt like all the baggage was gone, just like when I was a child. The absolute truth is at the core of our relationship and once more was real love. All the anxiety and expectations, met and unmet, disappeared. The love between a father and a son is once again free. This sensation washed over me as I sat next to his hospital bed and read to him.

The feeling of peace filled my heart — the moments in my life when I have had let go of all of my own expectations and have immersed myself in the comfort, peace, and love God has for me.

I have been told by a friend that how I view my earthly father greatly influences how I see my heavenly father.

As a small boy, I saw no blemish on my father, and then changing worlds took another perspective or place inside our relationship.

Twenty-four years have now passed since I have felt free of all burdens when in his presence.

As a little boy, I would lie on his chest, look onto his face, and poke at his nose. I would move his cheeks with my fingers and feel the scruff of his beard. Today, as a 35-year-old man, I found myself doing this again as he lay there in bed. All of a sudden, I feel like the little boy, and he feels like my dad. He feels like my Superman.

At 35, I remembered what it was like to emotionally feel like Dad was my Superman

Journey of the Son

once more. I have read that love is the ultimate healer. He needed his son's love. I wanted to give my love. As I look back on the moment, part of the reason why I felt secure is that he was not strong enough to hurt me. Rather, he needed us, his family. He was in no position to be full of pride. The risk of his rejecting my love with his tongue or hand was not there.

What happens when the curtain is torn? Where do we go? What do we do? What do we think?

At the age of 9, my father struck me for the first time out of anger. It shook me. Then, by the time I was 11, the abuse came more frequently until home became a battle ground. By the time I was 14, the last time I remember feeling my dad's love, it had all but disappeared for me.

I started to feel alone in this world. Questions flooded my mind. You mean to tell me my dad is not Superman? He makes mistakes? The questions answered themselves. He will play a major role in bestowing to me emotional pain. He is not my protector from this world. Instead of my Superman he is now Lex Luthor, my nemesis.

Marcus Santi

I am a runner. God blessed me with the ability to run, to sprint. I learned to hurdle by the age of 9. By the time I was 11, I had run one lap around the track in under 60 seconds. Later in my life, I was able to combine those two skills: 400m (meter) running and hurdling. Life itself is a hurdle.

When you line up in the starting blocks of an actual 400mh race you are going to face four constants: 10 hurdles, distance between the hurdles, hurdle height, and the distance of the race.

The 400mh (meter hurdle) race is labeled as the toughest race in track and field; if you can win in this environment you can win in any environment. Let's find out what it takes to become a champion in such circumstances

Here is a game plan laid out for me by the world record holder in the event; this was his game plan as he set the world record in 1992. You treat the first three hurdles like you would a 400m race: no hurdles – you just get them out with aggression and speed. You are going to flatten out your stride a bit and push forward with the hips moving in a flat plain of movement. Think of a line graph – the line is following the hips and there will not be a lot of vacillating movement at the hip. The foot contact is really pushing you forward.

Now after hurdle 3, you are getting "settled in" to the race. You're finding the "groove." You lighten up on the gas pedal just a bit, conserving energy, though you really aren't loosing much speed – you just aren't pushing for additional speed at this phase of the race. You hold this pattern until you get to hurdle 5, then you open up the stride a little bit more. Your stride becomes bouncy, but not too bouncy. You're like an antelope at this stage of the game, real light on your feet. This allows you to regain and prepare for your final push to the finish line. At this stage, you are halfway through the race. You execute this for two hurdles and now after hurdle 7, which is in the middle of the turn on most tracks, you make your charge back into the race.

You have about 145Mm and you start building your speed up into hurdle 8; this is where the men and the boys are separated. This hurdle tells you a lot about who is going to win and who is going to fold. After hurdle 8, as you are heading into hurdle 9 and 10, it's all about the *want to*! It's about how much guts you have and how well you can manage the pain. The *want to* is your will to win and to finish strong.

At hurdle 8, how do you become strong enough to deal with the rest of the race? What you are really addressing is the question of what happens when the stuff hits the fan in life – when all the distractions are taking you away from your focus. How do you combat this? In the race, it is dependent on what you have done in your preparatory work leading into that moment: **"It is not the will to win; it is the will to prepare to win."**

In the off-season, how much time in the weight room did you put in? How many of those stadium steps or hills did you run? How many 500m and 600m sprints did you run in practice? And then there is the balance between the pure speed work and the endurance training needed to complete this race. There is still a performance standard an athlete desires to attain. There has to be an appropriate balance of how you train your body. An athlete has to find a way to make weakness into strength. You must find the balance to attain your optimal race – your prescription for an optimal life.

I have found it exhausting: the worry of stressing out over my race game plan. I grew to hate that aspect of the 400mh. I was not allowing myself to just run. I was letting the hurdles dictate the way I ran my race; I couldn't let myself flow and simply race. I became trapped inside the distance between the hurdles. I remember something a teacher/coach would tell me: "You learn all of this so that you can forget it." She was telling me, let yourself go. Trust that you know it. Let it become instinctive. Live from your insides.

My instincts have led me to triumphs; my ego has led me to downfalls. Over time, I learned what to listen to and what to ignore. I learned where my deficiencies were and then developed courage to face them. These were the things I feared and hated to do, but must do in order to run my best race and live my best life. Eventually, I started to love them – I loved what they did for my race: how they made me a better runner and gave me the ability to compete for wins.

Come race day, there are so many factors that are out of a runner's control. It doesn't matter. All the competitors have to face to the same factors.

In order to optimize training, it helps to be part of a great environment. The environment I practice and compete in plays a great role in determining how fast or slow my performance time is. There are training groups, and the zest is either just not there or it is all there. Which group is going to allow me to attain my best time? What environment is going to allow me to live my best life? What friends? What girlfriend? What job? What city? All of this plays a role as to how the best ME will come forward.

Here are two golden nuggets I have heard as an athlete or a coach. First, "Know that you know that you know." Second, "How 'bout you run as fast as you need to in order to win?" Wow! What a great idea! These two nuggets allow me to transcend beyond the barriers I form in my mind that limit my speed and my ability. When I "know that I know that I know," this allows me to run a stress-free race. I found out that the race is truly not that difficult. Instead, it is the mountains I made them out to be. The race, and life more broadly, is an effort – a big FOCUSED effort – but it can be done without killing yourself. The stress I brought to the race was killing me on the last 100m. The stress I brought to the race was draining my energy in the warm up area before the starter pistol ever went off. The race is supposed to be fun. So is life.

Journey of the Son

The reason why the 400mh is labeled the toughest race in track and field: it will fold you in half if you are not strong enough for it. It will make you cry; it will make you feel like you have died but are still alive. It's something for the strong of heart. If you have any doubts, it will expose them. It will crush you. Is life not the same way?

Life, a fulfilled life, is not for the faint of heart. We must face our fears if we are going to experience the glory that is out there. It takes courage to do the things we should do even though we don't want to do them. Those are the 500m sprints and setting up the last 100m of that sprint with three hurdles. Those efforts set us up for the win – for the personal best efforts. We must have courage to go after accomplishments that most see as unfeasible. We must have discipline to make ourselves run with a "grade A" effort so we can overcome anything the race may throw at us. Why do I do it? It is good for me. It keeps my edges sharp and ready. All things in life have a balancing scale to them. Provided I keep the scale balanced in my effort, this is good for my life.

Marcus Santi

EVERY STEP YOU TAKE

When my dad started the abuse, I began to feel abandoned, abused, and eventually I felt rejected. I was a teen getting beat down emotionally and was gradually losing my courage and zest to go after the dreams of life. By the time my teen years started, I was better than anyone at putting myself down. "Beat 'em to the punch" was my motto. If I could reject myself first and make it into a jest, ultimately, in my mind, I couldn't be rejected by others. They could reject me, but I had put up a wall first so that I could protect myself from their rejection. It was as if I stepped away from my own body and said, "Let's make fun of that guy."

How does all this compare to life and abuse victims/ disadvantaged people? When I say victims/disadvantaged, I am not really saying you are at a disadvantage and for sure, we are not victims or have anything to do with a victim mentality. We may not have had a clean start to the first hurdle, but this does not prevent US from running the race. The fastest I have ever run the race, I almost fell on my face after the first hurdle and stumbled for three steps as I was trying to get myself upright and running again – quite indicative of my life's story. The

Journey of the Son

10 hurdles are still there and need to be cleared, just as in life. When things don't go your way or the way you feel they should go, compare an apple to an apple. Meaning, do what you do best and compare your effort and performance to past efforts. We all don't get cleanly out of the blocks; this doesn't mean the race is over. We still have a chance to get back on top of the race again. It is nice when we cleanly get out of the blocks and fire into the first hurdle, building momentum into the second hurdle.

Each of us is a child to someone. Some of us have gone on and become parents. Today's steps affect tomorrow's outcome. My first steps from the blocks can affect the outcome of hurdle 3. The coach has certain responsibilities to get the athlete ready for the race. When the gun goes off, there is nothing a coach can do anymore. It is entirely up to the athlete to "get 'r done." The prep work is 98 percent of the overall effort at hand. The coach has the ability to mentally, physically, emotionally, and even spiritually prepare the athlete for the rigors he or she will face in competition. The same is true with a parent as he or she prepares his or her child for the race of life.

How many have ever participated in a track

sprint race? (Field day counts.) It is nerve-wracking. In football, you're out there with 10 other guys along with a helmet and face mask that hides your face. In basketball, you have four teammates with you on the floor at all times. Track is an individual sport. At least, so it seems. It is just you in your lane and the competitors in their lanes. Everyone in the stands can see your face as clear as day. If you win, everyone can see your full identity (sans helmet, for instance). If you get dead last, everyone can see your face. Get it? You can't hide on that track behind teammates, a face mask, or an excuse like, "The coach didn't play me enough." Everyone gets their chance.

The team aspect comes into play behind the scenes. This is where most of the work it takes to win happens. Racing is only about 2 percent of what happens in an athlete's life. Who is there with the athletes the other 98 percent of the time? This includes the coach, friends, family, and teammates. Who you surround yourself with during these times greatly determines the outcome of how you will emotionally feel, physically perform, the confidence you will have, and your mental clarity come race time – during the 2 percent of your time. In a sprint race, you can blink and there is a good chance you cost yourself the race. You lose concentration, smash a hurdle, and you lose the race.

Remember the 2008 Olympics? There was an athlete on her way to gold, really close to a world record, but she flinched for a millisecond. It may have been doubt or loss of focus, but something affected her rhythm and her foot started to move too early and caught a hurdle. Her moment vanished in a millisecond.

Life: I'd say the first three hurdles are the stage of diapers to college. The starting blocks are the diapers stage, and by the time hurdle three hits, the race of adult life is about to begin. You leave home for the first time, you decide what direction you want to take in life, and you go and start making your own decisions that you will live by. It goes fast. Next thing you know, you are 40, 50, 60 years of age and you're getting into hurdle No. 8. I hope, for my sake, when I get to hurdle No. 8 of life I have a head full of steam, feeling like I am still in the middle part of my race, just flying over those hurdles.

There comes a point in time when it doesn't matter how your first three hurdles went in life. You are in the middle of the race. Now get a-running'. Go! Compete! If you're looking back at the three hurdles that didn't go so well, you're going to smash into the ones that are ahead of you.

If life is like a race, I know how keen my focus must be in order to execute the "perfect" game plan. Each step matters in this race. Parents, you are the coaches for your young ones. You have the responsibility to get them ready for the race of life. Your actions, how you live your life, and your decisions are being passed down to the ones you love. Maybe you don't love them. If that is the case, I can only say to you, "Let them be loved." Put them in a place which allows them to be loved. Sometimes, the best form of love is allowing someone else to provide the home and environment for the child to succeed and live his or her best life. This doesn't mean you don't love them.

For all of you adopted folks – your birth parents loved you and allowed you to be placed in a home that loves you hands-on. That is hard – to let go. I know because I have done it. I knew what was best for a child, and there will be a day when she will want to know who I am and why I chose what I chose and my door will be wide open for her to ask. She will want a relationship, at least so, I hope. When she gets there, I will have confidence in knowing she had a good "first three hurdles."

Regardless of how well your "coach parent" has prepared you, the one thing you can control is your effort. Some of us have had great "coaches," and that gives us the best chance possible to run fast times. Regardless of our coaching, we all are going to run the race. It is up to the runner as to what kind of effort he or she will put forth. Your mindset going into the competition and your attitude matters. The people in the stands, the ones who truly know competition, will root for you no matter what place you are in.

Teddy Roosevelt said it best: "It is not the critic who counts, not the man who points out how the strong man stumbles, or where the doer of deeds could have done them better. The credit belongs to the man who is actually in the arena, whose face is marred by dust and sweat and blood; who strives valiantly; who errs, who comes short again and again, because there is no effort without error and shortcoming, but who does actually strive to do the deeds; who knows great enthusiasms, the great devotions; who spends himself in a worthy cause; who at the best knows in the end the triumph of high achievement, and who at the worst, if he fails, at least fails while daring greatly, so that his place shall never be with those cold and timid souls who neither know victory nor defeat."

Parents, be a safe haven for your child. We all are going to bang into a hurdle. Don't be a hammer telling us how we hit the hurdle. Treat the wound, disinfect the cut, pick us up if we need it, and show us how to get over that hurdle again and again. Do it with your actions.

I am a believer in actions, not words. My dad failed in many ways with his words and his actions. They inflicted wounds. It didn't build my self-esteem, but took it from me. Eventually, it was a fight for me at home. My guard was always up. It took energy from me. I had already run three races by the time I walked out the door of my home to get to the starting blocks of life. That is my past, and it has determined who I am today. I have "fight" in me; it was just the way I was raised in my teen years. At times, it seems as though this fight is engrained in my psyche. I try within the walls of my heart, mind, and soul to bring peace to myself. If I am at peace within my walls, I can bring peace and love to those outside my walls. What I give in life is what I will receive back.

Some call it karma. What I see and what I hear is greatly affecting what I say and do. The EYES AND EARS are the gateway to the soul. What I feed them determines my thought life. My thought life plays out in my physical life.

You Are Not Alone

A hope for this book is to allow the abused to understand they are not the only ones out there. You are not by yourself.

I heard a man speak of lions hunting in Africa. They are often not fast enough to run down their prey. Instead, it is a hunt of precision and purpose. The lions hunt together. They can identify the weak prey. Eventually, they start to separate the weak from its pack. There is protection for the prey if they stay in their pack. The lions will get between the pack and the weak. The other lions encircle the prey and devour it.

The man was saying this is how evil/negativity can get you. It separates you from the pack and gets you to think you are the only one. Then, when it has you worn down and separated, it hops on you and takes you down. This is what happened to my father. He got separated and he made a bad decision.

Healing is possible. There is opportunity for you to work your way through the hurt and find health within your soul. Set yourself free from the abuse and abusers in your life. The abuser in your life can be lying in wait just inches from you in bed every night. If you have freedom in your heart and in your mind, you have freedom. The body will heal. The soul will heal as well.

We all have been told, "No." To what extent and how it has been told to us is part of our story, too. We all have a story in ourselves. Some have experienced extreme abuse – verbal abuse, physical abuse, and/or mental abuse. Life, as I mentioned, is like a hurdle race. When the hurdles start to get in our way, are we going to run at life's obstacles full speed – learning how to skim right over the top and keep moving to the next hurdle with speed and fluidity – or are we going to stop running? It's our choice.

It's The Small Things

When I was a kid, I had dreams – big dreams. I didn't have the kind of dad who passed on to me appropriate building blocks to take me to "the promised land." I needed emotional support. He was not there for me in my teenage years. This was my major motivation as an adult to start coaching. I didn't intend on becoming a coach; it literally fell into my lap. Where he lacked in teaching me I was forced to go and find out on my own if I wanted to know the answer. This made me into a great coach.

My family in general is blessed with the ability to teach. We are teachers. My Aunt Rita is a great teacher, my dad was a great teacher in the mortgage business, and my cousin John is a leader in his field. The other quality we have in our family is a big heart. My grandmother and my Aunt Dodie have the biggest hearts I know. The entire aforementioned have a great care for their respective subjects. The big heart is what makes us great at our teaching.

I would consider myself a great teacher. My care for others combined with an ability to teach caused me to understand the importance of others achieving their goals. The absence of what I should have felt from my father allowed me to understand how important it is to give others the support and the chance to find their dreams – and not only find them, but make them a reality.

It is a wonderful thing to look into a child's eyes. When humans are young, they do not know how to put up the wall to not let you in to see their heart. This is why coaching and parenting can be so fulfilling; this is what makes it precious. You can either build up or tear down a soul when a child allows you to see it. I have flashbacks to all the times a child has looked at me and allowed me to invest some of my philosophies into their lives. I think it is a good thing to allow someone to see past the walls we build up as human beings.

I will share a story of one of the many athletes I had a chance to train. I definitely felt like I was part of the family. The parents of the athlete accepted me and let me implement my teachings. This athlete was a great competitor, and I was fortunate to be around great competitors throughout my coaching career. This athlete was all heart – one of those types that wore everything on her sleeve.

This young girl – I will never forget our second high school track meet. She was in the 8th grade and was talented enough to be moved up to compete at the highest level that high school offered – varsity level. It was the regional track championship meet. The next level of competition was the State Championships, which you qualify for if you place in the top two in the race.

The event was the 300mh. Keep in mind, this girl was a late bloomer. She was about 5'1" and weighed less than 95lbs. In this race was the reigning regional champion and regional record holder. I guided my protégé through the warm up. I believe in a good thorough warm-up, though most athletes do not grasp this concept.

As she is about to go over to the starting line, she stops and looks up at me and remarks, "Marcus, I'm scared. Do you think I will win?" I looked her squarely in her eyes and said to her "No matter what happens in this race, your mother and father are still going to love you. Nothing you do in this race will change how I think about you. Just give it your best." She looked up at me and smiled. I was saying it doesn't matter whether you win or lose, I am still so very proud of you and the outcome of this race is not going to change a thing.

She looked back at me and this huge grin came across her face, which was full of braces, I might add. I knew for the moment she had peace. When that happens, the athlete is free to run. The gun went off and she went on to do what she does best. She ran like a god and demolished the field. She not only demolished the regional champion, she demolished the regional record as well: the previous record was 49 seconds and she ran 47 seconds. At the finish line there was this PIG TAILED girl – and then the rest of the field about 20 yards behind her. All of this was possible because she trusted with her heart. She flew like an eagle. When I look back, the best moment was seeing peace on her face and in her heart. The by product was a region record and victory.

Heart

With all of the athletes I coached, I coached their hearts. I knew how successful my heart made me as an athlete. It allowed me to transcend a lot of barriers my mind put on my body when I let it. I was successful only when I trusted and believed what my heart wanted more than what my fear was prohibiting me from.

I believe in synergy. I cannot achieve synergy when I am on my own. It really doesn't matter if I let myself down. If one has the hope of others in the heart, the heart will compete in a miraculous fashion. I will die with effort trying to get victory because of those in my heart; I want to give it to them. I guess that I am a pleaser. Doesn't winning make the party better? It makes everyone part of something when you bring them along.

Fear keeps us caged, confuses us, and keeps us from finding our true hearts – the people God made us to be. It takes courage to stand against the current just so we can find who we are, if that is what it takes.

Love – real love, is boundless. Any person I have ever mentored or coached, my hope was always for them to find fulfillment. I fought for anyone I trained, anyone who wanted to live with passion, anyone who wanted to "mount up on wings like eagles and soar." Moreover, I wanted to see them soar. I wanted the team we formed to soar high above what we thought was possible. The 2003 track team that I coached achieved this. You know who you are and you are dear to my memories.

With the teams I coached, it was important to me and I thought it was necessary that we address the "invisible elephant" in the room. When the moment of truth comes out there on the athletic field, whatever we have not addressed has a way of coming back and haunting us. As a result of facing different issues, we won, performed our best in championship meets and during stressful situations, and all became better people as well.

If it meant that I had to expose my heart, I would do what I needed for truth to be found. I would risk breaking the façade, breaking what the athletes thought of me. I would let them know I was a human just like them. I would let them know that we were all in it together. They would know that there wasn't a wall that separated them from me even though I was their coach. It made for very powerful moments, and there were some athletes who would not perform for others, but they would give their all when I asked it of them. I think truth wins out. Truth wins over false pride and false glory.

I let them know there was a risk of failure. We prepare for our success. We become the best we can be on and off of the playing field. We face the fears within ourselves. No matter how ugly the truth may look, we shared it.

A true team becomes a safe haven from the outside world and the outside forces that tell us that we are going to fail. Norms and "realists" tell us we need to "behave this way so we can fit into society." Any team I was a part of, I endorsed bringing your personality to the "party." And, I've been blessed to experience many wonderful personalities. I have seen many laughing faces, many angry faces, sad faces, and jubilant faces. This is what happens when we allow people to fully be themselves: we get all of them; we experience the real human being that they are.

Chapter 2

An Olympiad of Time

Every four years, there is an Olympics. In Ancient Greek times, 4-year increments were called Olympiads. It started at the beginning of the year, January 1st, in which the Summer Olympics were held. To me, this is one of the reasons why the Olympics are the greatest celebration sport can offer. Four years of waiting between competitions for what could possibly be the moment you were born for. Some go on to worldwide glory, and some go on to attain only personal glory. Anyone who is able to attend and participate experiences the glory of the Olympic Games.

To explain how much passion an Olympic athlete has, one can reference a survey given years ago to athletes striving to make the Olympics. The survey asked, "If you could take a pill that would guarantee you Olympic Gold, but you would die from it in five years, would you take it?" This is called Goldman's Dilemma. You can Google it. How many do you think said "Yes"? Over half said they would take it. This is a poll taken from the 1970s to the mid-90s. This is the era of time I grew up in and competed.

The Goldman's Dilemma illustrates how much passion an Olympic athlete can have. This is how much passion it takes to live a life questing for a moment that can only exist for a day. All your life for one day – for 10 seconds if you are a 100m runner. Do you understand what that means? Everything you have ever breathed, it comes into a slow motion replay for the rest of your life. Whether you experience triumph or tragedy, it is something you will play over and over in your mind. It can drive you to your success or your ruin. It is up to you and how you play it greatly determines the outcome. Do you not think Ben Johnson does not think about his moment every day of his life? Lolo Jones, if she could have it back, would in an instant. Dan Jansen was down to his last Olympic effort ever and came up with a world record in an event that was a secondary effort. These are moments that live with all of us who are called. When the flags are flying and we see and hear the national anthem…if you get tears in your eyes, then you understand. It is passion at its greatest. It is an athlete at his or her greatest. It is the agony of defeat and the thrill of victory which only comes around once an Olympiad. For some, an Olympiad is once in a lifetime. This is how I feel.

Sometimes, I find myself trying to numb out when I see this type of glory because my opportunity has come and gone. Every time I hit the track, I love to find my glory. I love to feel this passion. I am not searching for any Olympic glory, I'm just searching for the glory within myself. This is another reason why I try so hard at what I attempt. I have to fight the hurt within. All the hurt is doing is keeping me from my glory. It just hit me, I forget what it is to have all that passion rattling around in my soul. It is refreshing when I feel it again. I sometimes suppress my passion because I question myself, "What happens if I don't make it?" "What happens if I fail?" Without trying I will never know what it is to make it. Without risk I will never appreciate the accomplishment. What happens if I live a life and never know what it is like to be scared out of my mind, to face it down, and find out the glory residing in me is greater than the fear residing in me? What if I find out I am an overcomer, that I am great?

The only way we can find our greatness is if we dare to dream and go after those dreams with all of our mind, body, soul, and HEART.

Athletes today, when presented with Goldman's Dilemma, responded with a very low number of "yes" answers. Let me ask: How many athletes in today's world are still getting hit with 4-game bans in the NFL? The Tour de France: Why did no other rider get awarded the Tour De France title when Lance Armstrong was stripped? All of them were testing positive as well. How many guys who are running under 10 seconds in the 100m are getting hit with drug suspensions? Check it out – they all get caught at some point in time. It makes me wonder if any of them are doing it legally.

I accept that there are some people truly born to be athletes. There are some of us and we, well, have our moments. I think of a human body like that of Bolt; he is an oddity. I have never seen a man that tall able to drive out of the blocks like he can. It is a given that once he gets those long legs unfolded and running, the rest of the field is in trouble. So, maybe he is an alien mix breed or something. The rest of the guys, they're not 6'5" with the legs of a 7-foot man. I have run next to some really, really fast men. I don't know how the human body can run as fast as these guys are running.

Maybe at some camp the answers were low, but they are still taking performance enhancing drugs more than ever. I hate to tell the public this, but open your eyes. Yes, training has gotten better and it starts at an earlier age, but have we really advanced that much? Mark McGuire and Sammy Sosa – baseball took their hit when those guys got busted and supposedly they implemented a testing policy to win the fans back. But, guys are still just as big as those two were. When money is in the game, palms get greased and heads are turned the other way because everyone is making a dollar off of it and the fan is none the wiser. Most cheaters, for the most part, are only remorseful after they have been caught. The athletes and coaches know who the "dirty ones" are. I think we accept it as part of the business. As a coach, it comes down to the pressure of winning or not winning. It is one thing if a coach was to tell an athlete to take performance enhancing drugs and it is another to turn the other way when you see it.

When you are an athlete and you want something badly, all face forks in the road.

Some are moral forks. Some are legal forks. I was faced with my extreme desire to run a particular time in the 400 hurdles and now Goldman's dilemma began for me. Each athlete has to lay their head on their pillow at night and know what he or she has sacrificed to reach those goals. I was faced with the steroids dilemma. I had an athlete approach me and share how he used steroids coming off an injury. He told me he came back stronger and better. He believed Vit-S did help him hit new levels with his body which allowed him to be better at his sport. It wasn't like he was an avid user. He did one cycle (6 weeks) to help him recover from an injury. By doing this, it took his game to another level. He simply shared with me the benefits he personally experienced. He said, "I see how hard you work at your sport. It will help you get to the next level." I thought about it long and hard. We all have friends who have taken sports enhancing drugs. Back in the 1980s, 90s, and early 2000s, you got the Vit-S through a friend. I had a friend who could get me Winstrol V. This was something sprinters would use. I had a bottle of Winstrol V in my face and $200 in my hand. I decided not to buy the Vit-S. I bought his computer instead and let my girlfriend at the time use it (which I never

Journey of the Son

saw again when I got back from my training camp in Tallahassee).

It was more about not knowing how to use this drug than it was about whether it was legal or not. I didn't really know how to use the drug and when to use it. There is a certain time in training when it is most helpful and there are times when it is not. The Russians have it down to a science, literally.

I passed the test. I said no to the drugs. I don't know what other athletes are doing today and really it is none of my business. I do know that every Tom, Dick, and Harry has the opportunity to go to the corner drug store and get his steroid shots at a LOW T Center (a place anyone can walk in and get a shot of steroids). This pertains to non-athletes. Low T centers are here to recapture our youth supposedly. When athletes use performance enhancing drugs it is usually to make an income for them. Which is worse? Which is immoral? Don't cast the first stone.

An athlete in today's world is somewhat like a corporation. He has a whole staff around him; he has an agent, personal trainer, personal chef, public relations personnel, shoe/clothing company, and a massage therapist (who is usually extremely attractive and so is the nutritionist). The nutritionist is completely different than the personal chef. Chefs can cook; the nutritionist just looks good and tells you what you need to eat.

When the athlete/corporation gets injured, the "corporation" takes whatever measure is needed to get your butt back in the best shape of your life so the organization that is paying you millions gets their dollar value out of you. Wow, I hope I haven't snuffed out your childhood fantasy about athletes now. They're humans just like you.

In my day, we played for blood, for bragging rights to the neighborhood. If you got knocked down, you got right back up. If you were bleeding, you wiped it off on your pant leg and tried to find the guy who did it, and made sure he got his. And, by the way, this wasn't in some video Gameboy land. We actually physically did these things with our own bodies.

So now you know what I believe when it comes to athletics and what it takes to be an athlete, a real athlete. We have too many corporations/businesses and men/athletes walking around in today's athletic world. I like my tough guys. The "no nonsense," "stick in your face," play hard "Dennis Rodman" type of guys.

The human body, outside of a few, has a small window of opportunity for peak performance, the level of performances that will keep you on top of your sport. An Olympiad of time is a lifetime for most athletes. Within a 4-year span they will have one real shot at claiming Olympic glory: a life-long journey has a possibility inside a 4-year window. For me, when looking at any Olympic experience, an athlete qualifying for the Olympics is glorious. It is something I felt called toward. As I stated earlier, I think without a doubt it is the purest and most glorious experience in all of athletics.

I once trained an MLS player. He was an all-star in that league. I asked him, "At what level HAVE you enjoyed your sport the most?" He was in the midst of a contract dispute and was sitting out for a spell until the contract could get worked out. This is a guy who was part of a national championship in high school and college. He experienced winning at those levels. Now he is in the pros and in a dispute with the organization over his pay. He said to me, "Without a doubt, where I am right now [professional] is the most fun I am having. I am able to play amongst the best and find out how good I can be." Even with all that is out there to taint professional sports, there are still the athletes who remember what it is to be a kid and play in the backyard for blood and bragging rights.

I think that for the sake of sports it is important to remember why we first started playing. Professional sports have a way of weeding out those who are not doing it for the right reasons. It is too hard to go through the training, the ups and the downs that come with athletics, to do it for the money. After a while it is just too much. And this is also why I say the Olympics are the greatest/purest effort in sport. For two weeks, no one cares about all the political bull that is going on in the world. We care about the human spirit. We cry when we see our flag raised. We remember all those days on the practice field/track. We remember for a moment that there is hope in this world. I know for me, when I saw my bib as I competed in the Masters World Champions of Track and Field that it stated USA on the bib, not my name. I am running for something greater than my name. I am running for hope, for an idea that I believe God instills in us. We compete and give it our all because we want our home to be a better place. The human spirit in an Olympic effort is the human condition at its finest. It is what makes our species great.

Chapter 3

Runners to Your Mark

I come from a divorced household, where my parents were apart from birth. I never knew what it was like for them to live under the same roof – never knew what it was like for them to share a kiss. I only knew what it was like for two war machines to collide every Friday and Sunday evening (to pick me up and drop me off). For those who are not familiar with divorced households, one of the parents gets visitation. This was the 1970s, so it was very unheard of for the father to have the child during the week. I lived with my mother during the week and my father came and got me on the weekends.

My dad would come pick me up every Friday. For the most part, dad was like a big teddy bear to me. He was tons of fun. He would usually come pick me up in the TR6. It was always fun, fun, fun when he showed up in the TR6. Dad was really good at hyping up stuff. I remember when we were going to see Star Wars. He said, "Son, there is a spaceship and it moves at the speed of light!" He would go over to a lamp and make sure that the room was completely dark. "Are you watching? Are you watching?" I was in amazement, "Yeah, I'm watching." He would turn the light on. "Did you see that – how fast the light went through the room? That's how fast this spaceship moves!" I just had the biggest eyeballs in anticipation to see this lightning fast spaceship. We jumped in the TR6 and pulled a Millennium Falcon as we jumped to light speed to the theater…except we were in a British sports car.

My godlike dad would drag race with me as a 5 year old, in the car. He used to love racing cars and did so often when he was 19 to 23 years old. He had a souped-up '56 Chevy and I got to hear story after story about how fast his car was. One time in the TR6 we were at a stop light and we took on his good friend Larry Crawford in his '67 Corvette. Dad did some things with this straight line 6 cylinder to make it move a little faster. As we were at the red light, I knew by the way he was revving the engine that we were about to hit it. "You ready?

Journey of the Son

Hang on." And bam! We were gone. We raced all over that town – Memphis. He was crazy, but crazy in a way that I loved. It scared me a little at times, but I learned to love the adrenaline as it shot through my body. My nose would tingle sometimes. Anytime there were curves, dad took full advantage of the car's ability to hug the road and would burn through the turns. It was always fun. I was his partner in crime; we were the best of buddies. He was my Superman. He was my best friend. I had so much fun with my dad during those years.

As a result of this upbringing, by the time I was 15 years old I had driven over 100 miles per hour....with dad in the car. He took me out to a country road. Dad always justified our daredevil activities by saying, "I want you to know how to do it right." He supervised my dare deviling, beer drinking, and cigar smoking activities. When he said to me in the car, "You want to hit it?" My eyes got so big – YES I DID! We came to a halt and he let me run through the gears. It was 0 to 100 as fast as I could get there. I caught rubber changing from first to second and the car went a tad sideways, but I was in control. As he told me to back off of it and I came off the accelerator, Dad was laughing and just rubbed my head. "Yup, a chip off the old block," he said.

By the time I was on the road legally, I really didn't know how to drive slowly. I would classify myself as a good driver. I was just a really good driver at high rates of speed. My brain worked better there. I was quick with good reflexes. My mind thought quickly, "As a man thinketh so he becomes," right? Well, in this case we are going to say "Yes." I am still alive and so are others on the road.

We were daredevils. This one time, when I was about 8, we went down to Destin, Fla. This was an annual trip. There was a hurricane out in the Gulf of Mexico; there was beautiful weather on the beach, but it was sending huge, and I mean huge, waves into shore. They were the biggest I had ever seen. So what did we do? We went to the store and buy a Styrofoam board so we could ride some waves. Guess what? The board broke in half. We went back to the store and got a canvas raft and goggles.

We were out in those waves waiting and waiting for the biggest to ride. Dad was holding me and getting me ready on the raft and as a wave came, he insisted, "Paddle! PADDLE PADDLE!" Dad would push me, helping me catch the wave. Those waves sent me twirling

Journey of the Son

like I was in a washing machine – that is, if I didn't ride it like a bull rider all the way into the shore! We would celebrate every successful wave. After an unsuccessful ride, we got the raft prepared for the next successful ride, and very quickly at that. I had bruises and a little blood by the day's end – but who cares! There was fun to be had.

I do remember this one time where even dad got a little scared, but he kept it together and pulled us through. I was about 5 and he would always take me bike riding. He would put me in the seat that he put on the back of his 10-speed and away we went for an adventure. This particular time, we were out at Shelby Forest, and there were some big hills out there! The daredevil in my dad got going again. We started charging down this hill like we were in le Tour de France going down the mountainside of the Pyrenees. I was on the back screaming my ass off, telling him to stop. All I could hear were the wheels humming – we were going so fast. When we were going around the bends, we were leaning so far toward the ground that I could have reached out and scraped it with my hand. This scared me into looking three shades of white. We got to the bottom and I was crying. He had the big smile on his face and a little crazy in his eyes. Laughing, he said, "Yeah, that was scary. I did bite off a bit more than I could chew. I got into it and I just had to go with it. I just couldn't stop." We could have died on that one, but we didn't.

He would take me on his dates sometimes. We did a combo job this one time. While dad was making out with the mom, I was in the back bedroom with the daughter. I was about 10. I will never forget how the daughter told me to come back to her bedroom and to get under the bed while she undressed herself in front of me. If the daughter was doing this with me who knows what the mom was doing with dad! Yup, the Santi clan had been to that house!

I loved my dad. My mom will tell me to this day that he was the most fun she has ever had on a date. She will also let me know that as much fun as he was on a date, he was that bad as a husband. Well, there aren't many of us grading out with an "A" in all categories of life. I know I haven't.

When my mother reads the above, she will wonder what she was thinking by subjecting her child to this behavior. Mom, I turned out all right…kind of sort of. To mom's saving grace, she was able to remarry and stay married. This

Journey of the Son

somewhat "tamed" her. She's still kind of crazy though. Many people who know my parents from way back when will tell me, "I can't believe you turned out as sane as you are with the parents you have." My two aunts on my father's side are known as the "InSANTIty Sisters." It is not because they are mentally ill, although one of my aunts self-medicates with wine; she has it down to a science. It is because when they enter a room, they are instant entertainment. They were and to this day are reality TV.

This is my family and the dynamics at work that helped form me. My grandmother was a card as well. She had the biggest heart of love I have ever known. There was this one time when a longtime employee, who was a black man, was doing some work on her house. She came out after he had fixed it all up and had done a really good job. She was so happy. When he left, my grandma would tell him how she loved him and would give him a bag of food to take with him. He would give my grandmother a hug and kiss on the cheek as well. She didn't care what race, religion, or creed you were. She looked beyond and saw with her heart.

This is the woman who raised the

"InSANTIty Sisters" and my crazy dad. She ended up raising me as well. What she did best was love with an open heart. My grandmother affected so many lives. All my friends enjoyed coming over to visit with Grandma. She fed you and really I think it was her way of giving love. Anyone who came in the door was going to either eat some pasta or her homemade cookies.

"LIKE FATHER LIKE SON"

How did Superman fall? What happened to us? To him? To me? If I experienced abuse then it would stand to reason that perhaps he experienced abuse. He did.

He would tell me how his father would hit him and call him a "bum." "You're going to be a bum. You're always going to be a bum." That is what my dad remembers his father telling him. His dad was from the "old country," Italy. He came over when he was 32 years old and married Josephine Anaratone at 34. He started his family then. In that day and age, that was late to be starting a family.

Italians are kind of fiery. We get passionate when we care about something, and we hardly ever show up on time. Have you ever tried to

Journey of the Son

get an Italian to dinner on time? See, we are on another time frame completely. It doesn't matter what time zone, we will get there eventually, and will have a bottle of wine with us. If you are a woman, yes, the males will enjoy your presence and let you know how beautiful you are. It is just in our DNA, sorry. If you don't believe me ladies, go date one. You will never have another lover that you will hate and love more. It is masterful how we can do this. I don't know how it is done, we just are this way.

The unrestrained passion my grandfather had somehow led him to hit my dad. He hit, and dad was left with these memories of abuse. He couldn't let go of it. All of his life, he tried to prove to his father that he wasn't a bum. I found it ironic that even after his father had passed, he worked relentlessly to prove he wasn't a bum to a man who was in the ground. Isn't it amazing the haunting – or beneficial – memories our parents can leave to us? We give them the ability to breathe life into us and we also give them the ability to give our joy or take our joy. As we mature, we have more awareness of this becoming our choice in whom or what we let give or take our joy. The joy comes from within us. The sadness comes from within us. As a man thinketh, so he becomes.

For me, it took stepping away from a busy life to get quiet and still so I could deal with God and with myself. I had too many negatives shooting around within my mind. It takes courage and a deliberate effort to stop running from yourself and turn to face the shadow following you. My shadow drove me to success by a relentless will and a touch of insecurity as I strove to prove myself worthy of being loved. My dad has a big heart, something he got from his mother that has been passed on to me. A big heart is the greatest thing on earth: it will drive us to greatness because we can only live with the contentment of knowing we did our best. We gave our best to others. When a heart becomes fragmented and skewed, it is dangerous where it can land, what it can lead one to do.

My father's heart got skewed. He put a bullet in his head. My heart started to become skewed, and I stopped before I put a bullet in my head. When I saw my father lying in ICU with bandages wrapped around his head, eyeballs about to pop out of his skull, head oblong shaped from the swelling, I nearly passed out. As I laid my own eyes on a suicide attempt, a suicide attempt gone wrong, it cured me. I thought for the longest time that I was a suicide waiting to happen. I was just biding my time before I put the bullet in my own head.

With my own eyes, I saw what suicide does to a family. It was not a successful one, but it changed all of our lives. It is selfish to do this to your family and to those who love us. Oh God, how it hurt to see my Superman lying in bed fighting for his life, fighting the demons within that left him with the resolution that a bullet to the brain was easier than seeing another sunrise on this planet, another wave in Destin, a beautiful woman lying by his side as he would sleep, and to see the smile on his son's face.

Chapter 4

VINCERO VINCERO VINCERO

During my father's recovery, the extended family had gathered to check on my two aunts and me, as we were caring for Dad, and we were updating them on his progress. Together, we were all wrestling with why he would commit such an act. Life does go on and we, as a family, would travel through this together.

This catastrophic event jerked all of us out of our ordinary worlds to some degree, but for me, everything had changed. For over two years I had planned to go to Italy to compete in the World Masters Athletics Championships in September 2007. For those unfamiliar with European terms, "athletics" equates to "track and field." This meet attracts over 9,100 athletes from all over the world.

In a mere moment all of my plans had changed. Upon hearing the news of my father, I left my home and work in California to be at Dad's side in Memphis.

Trusting God is something in my life I have struggled with often. To trust we must let go of anxiety and fear of an undesired outcome. When I let go of my expectations it is easier for me to find the best answer for the situation. Most people who believe there is a God would classify this as God leading them. The decision that God's way is better than my way does not come easily for me. It's been hard for me to trust; this is something in my life that has been dramatically changing for the better.

I wanted to go to Italy very badly. I let go of my control for the desired outcome to go to Italy. I did continue to train for the competition. I had a faith the competition in Italy could still become a reality. California is where I thought my life was supposed to be. I was only supposed to stay in Memphis for a week. My wants and desires for MY life was there in California.

I had my crossroad; stay in Memphis or go back to California? I could have sought revenge on my father once more and left him there. My anger could have driven my thoughts. I let go of MY life. I knew what I needed to do to have my

Journey of the Son

life be my own: I didn't care what my father had done to me. He was lying in a bed with a bullet wound because of the bed he made for himself. I knew what he needed. I knew what would heal my father. He loved me and I knew it. He loved the thought of his son. His son being by his side through all of this was more valuable to Albert Santi, my father, than any medicine or treatment he could have received. He desired and needed love. I chose to forego my control to travel to Italy to compete. I let go and trusted. I guess I trusted God and the circumstances that had been given to me. I stayed in Memphis….by my father's side.

After many weeks of being with Dad, my family had gathered together on a Sunday night in Memphis to reflect on all that had happened, and my hope to make the competition in Italy was running thin. My departure date was fast approaching, less than a week away. I did have a plane ticket by way of a buddy pass, but with an empty bank account it seemed traveling to Italy would be absolutely impossible.

Then, we were introduced to Paul Potts.

My cousin, Regina, had seen a video online, and wanted to share it with the family. The family is of Italian decent, so opera is very familiar to us. We all gathered in the study around a computer screen to watch a video of an audition for the British television show *Britain's Got Talent*. As the video started, a short, pudgy, crooked toothed man (who works in a cell phone warehouse) gets up to perform before three judges, including Simon from *American Idol*.

They asked, "What do you want to do?"

He replied, "I want to sing opera." You could see the judges roll their eyes. What proceeded from that point was unbelievable.

As this man, Paul Potts, sang the song "Nessun Dorma," everyone was captivated. He embodied beauty as he sang a simply tremendous rendition of the song.

What was most spectacular was that in the eyes of our culture, this man was "a frog" – a man with no looks and no presence. He was someone to be discarded. However, in reality this ordinary man was a knight with shining armor. Tears filled the eyes of the audience (and in our room) as we listened to Paul Potts sing.

Personally, I wanted to put my face into my hands and just let go of all my hurts and frustration. I wanted all the frustrations from

Journey of the Son

dealing with Dad – all the difficulties and pain to just pour out in tears. I couldn't cry. I think I was still in shock from all the events over the past two months. There was so much hurt. My aunts and I ached for wholeness. We wanted it to be over and better.

As I looked upon one of the most unlikely of men, Paul Potts, I saw a man, beaten up and discarded by the world, come through in absolute triumph as he sang.

The powerful audition ends with him repeating three times "Vincero, vincero, vincero!" ("I shall win! I shall win! I shall win!")

That night, God used Paul Potts to powerfully impact me – and my family. I do not know Italian, but the song gave me hope without even knowing the words. That night, the spirit of Paul Potts stirred our hearts and gave us hope – we shall win!

God used an unlikely series of difficulties and almost unbearable tragedy to bring our family together, and we responded as a family. Our hearts were stirred with hope and well-being.

My cousin, John Santi, sat with me and said, "Tell me about this track meet in Italy." He stepped up and invested himself in the effort. He became my financial sponsor, giving me a check, and helping me clear my last hurdle in the road to Riccione, Italy! His very words were, "I want you to go to Italy and make this family proud."

"Vincero, Vincero, Vincero!" "I shall win! I shall win! I shall win!"

Paul Potts went on to win *Britain's Got Talent* and I went on to Italy to give my all at the World Masters Athletics Championships. I had my chance to go to Italy.

I remember as my plane was approaching for landing I saw nothing but water. No land, just water. Eventually, out of nowhere, lily pads showed up. It was Venice. From high above, it looked like we were going to land on a lily pad. We touched down and I caught a water taxi to my place of stay. I was staying a stone's throw from St. Mark's Square. It is where all the pigeons congregate, the location you see in travel and tourism photos of Italy and with many pigeons in the same photo. Venice is unique. I have never been in a city like it. It is dark in its alley ways. It makes no sense in how it is designed.

Journey of the Son

This was a great high for me. I can remember that night; it was so beautiful there, seeing all of the cobblestone roads. Music was playing throughout the city. I heard Elvis being played. Isn't that awesome? I was thousands of miles away from my hometown of Memphis, a city known for the King of Rock and Roll, and I heard his song played.

I knew I would be eligible for this meet, and what a coincidence – my first time eligible to compete at the Masters World Championships and it was being held in the country my grandfather emigrated from; I was in my father's land.

Unbelievably, the last line of "Nessun Dorma", the Pavarotti hit sung by Paul Potts "At dawn, I shall win!" rang true for me. Within an hour of dawn Memphis time, our 4 x 400m relay team, on which I had the honor of running the final leg, went on to win the Silver Medal. If I would not have lived this, it would seem like a fairy tale.

Interestingly, while I did compete in an individual 400m race, I did not medal. My best performance was with the relay team. I beat my solo time by a full second and a half!

Marcus Santi

All my life, I have struggled with truly believing God has my best interest at hand. God used this experience during the summer of 2007 to confirm that 1) He does love me, 2) He does have the best for me, and 3) We are all in this existence together. No one is an island.

I have reached a mountaintop. The difference between this mountaintop and previous mountaintops is this one has many people living there. My previous mountaintops had just one resident – me. Today, I celebrate victory – a victory of many.

Many share in our family accomplishment, just as many have shared in the triumphant words of Paul Potts singing, "Vincero, Vincero, Vincero!"

"Vanish, o night! Fade, stars! At dawn, I shall win! I shall win! I shall win!"

I can remember speaking with my mom by phone, walking the cobble stone roads of a town in Italy as she told me how my father's actions hit her. She had been crying all day. She saw how Albert's actions affected her son, the one she loves. We were now in a moment of reprieve, yet we were all feeling it. It had been two months and I think we were just now

Journey of the Son

coming up for air.

My Aunt Dodie, the sweet tough one, told me how she had never cried through all of this. While I was gone, she told me how she was visiting her brother, and he was just lying there in the bed, unresponsive. If he would respond, it was possible that he could pass a test that would get him accepted into a top brain trauma rehabilitation facility. Aunt Dodie had high hopes for Albert's recovery. Finally, she broke. She laid her head on Albert's chest and broke into tears as she said to him, "Albert don't you want to get better? I need you. Marc needs you." She was just lying on him, crying, and she suddenly felt his hand on the back of her head rubbing her hair.

That was all my tough sweet little Aunt needed. Her hope came back to her. It was all coming out. We went through it as a family and we were healing as a family. We have our ways of finding healing.

The relationship I had with my father got so skewed away from the love he gave me as a child and was buried. It had been 24 years for me since I really felt the warmth of my dad's love and protection. I don't know how long it had been for him since he felt my love for him.

I don't know if he ever allowed himself to feel loved. One other valuable lesson I learned: I learned how to be my father's son.

No Excuses

I know there are some who pick up this book and say to themselves "Yeah, but...you don't...it must be nice to..." Where are the excuses in your life getting you? I am just asking. Ask yourself and take a good look at where you are. Where is your life going with your current thinking?

Yes, I know I am the one here looking to give out gold nuggets of advice, but there are some things that can be corrected. I have looked upon my life as a track race. It would be nice if all of us started a 100m race 100m away from the finish line. But I don't think that is the case with the human condition. There are some of us who come from outstanding mothers and fathers and our upbringing has been done right, or as best as it can be. And there are some of us who had a father and a mother who came from extreme abuse – whose parents had no idea how to love us, how to love each other, and for that matter, how to love themselves properly. In a lot of peoples' minds, this is what we would call a disadvantage. This is the equivalent of starting a 100m race 30m behind the start line.

We really don't know how to explode out of the starting blocks. What do we do to turn disadvantage over time into an advantage?

The translation into life occurs different ways. Often, people who get a great upbringing know how to behave inside of society. Discipline has been established. Emotional and financial support is provided for these types. When they have a question about life, all they have to do is call home and know they are getting great advice on how to deal with the unknown in their own life. The other types, the ones starting 30m behind everyone, have to figure it out on their own and hope they are getting it right. There is no one to call or so it feels. I have found there is always someone there to provide needed answers. It might not come from the source we desire most but it is an answer nonetheless.

I have found my trust in God and knowing that he will provide for me when I need it. This has brought me great calm and peace. Guess what – I might not have taken the road most traveled, but I am getting to my destination. This is the quantum jump I am referring to.

When we take the right paths, we leap forward beyond our competitors. I see no better trailblazer than the one who blazed the trail himself: God. How do I know it is God guiding me? That's a good question. It's one I have been trying to figure out for a while. Some days it is easy for me to know, others it is not. What I find is when my ego is in check it is easy to decipher whose voice is who's. Is it my ego voice or is it my higher self who is receiving the instructions laid out before me? I think somewhere inside of us all, we know when it is right, now it is a matter of following the right path.

In life, we compete against ourselves. Don't we all feel we have some destiny to fulfill? I know I do. I am at my best when I know in my heart that I am living my life at its fullest, completing my destiny. I am using the gifts that I have been given to make this world better.

When we were infants, we crawled. Then, we gained a little more strength and we walked. We got even stronger and we *ran* – we sprinted full speed. Get equipped. Become efficient with what you have. Identify your strengths. Work on your weaknesses. It takes a focused intention making the right choices in order to be your best. We can become very efficient at ignoring any vice or crutch we allow in our lives. That's the shadow that follows us.

The deficit we feel at the beginning can easily be made up later on in the race. When we figure out our strengths and weaknesses and embrace them for what they are, we start flying at warp speed. Our muscles start to work together instead of against one another. In sprinting, you have to let relaxation happen or the tensions of the muscles work against one another. You think you are running faster by straining with effort, but real speed comes when you let go of the tension and put the strength into the specific areas needed to propel you forward upon foot contact. The same is true with life. Put the focus into what you have. This will allow you to start achieving great results within your life. I believe the heartaches will ease and you will constantly be reinforcing to yourself your own strengths, as you will learn to use them to your advantage. Even your weaknesses will be more easily accepted, and with a gentle touch you can start to gain strength in areas you thought were lost causes.

How could I work on the areas of weaknesses? I would fast from the activity. I would take away what I had started to become most dependent upon. I do this a lot with my diet and with my exercise. I found out in a week's fasting period how reliant I had let myself become on my strengths. Just recently, I had the awesome opportunity to lose access to television and internet. Wow, did I become agitated! This opportunity offered me the chance to open other doors in my life. It allowed other dimensions of life to enter into my field of vision. Inspired by the Old Testament's Sabbath, having a day of rest after six days of work, –I decided to try working six weeks and taking one week of rest. I am an exercise aficionado and I really hate to take a week off. The healthiest I ever was, I abided by this philosophy for a year. I had no nagging injuries that year. It was the most I've ever weighed in my life while keeping a body fat percentage of less than 5%. I was strong and I was fast – 4.32 seconds fast in the 40 yard dash. This philosophy allowed me the opportunity to step back, address my weaknesses, repair, and move forward with more strength and balance. As much as I speak of the heart, sometimes the heart without discipline is a bad thing; this is the doubled-edged sword philosophy.

Journey of the Son

I WANT TO KNOW WHAT LOVE IS

Today, as an adult, my mom is one of my best friends. We did not start off that way for sure. Mom and I could fight vigorously. Our fights were probably how my dad and she fought, minus the physical abuse. We didn't physically abuse one another – we just tortured each other with our words. She would look at me with such disgust because not only was I stubborn like my father, I looked a lot like him. Can you imagine that? A man you want to absolutely forget, you have his son, and he looks just like him! You're telling me God doesn't have a sense of humor? There was some type of lesson to be learned in all of this for mom. If only I would have known then that I didn't have to say anything, that just my sheer presence was enough to win the fight...I might still have hair on top of my head!

How many of you can say, "My child is one of my best friends?" I want to congratulate you if you can. Something has gone right in your parenting. For those of you who cannot say this – there are some of you and you highly question why you had kids – hang in there; things change – just ask my mother.

Marcus Santi

When I was in my twenties, mom would often ask me for forgiveness. "Forgive me, Marc. I am sorry for not being there." Don't worry, we still had some epic fights during my twenties. She banned me from seeing my younger brother and I told her to go "F" herself and I took myself out of the equation for a whole summer. I love my brother very much. He is one of the foremost blessings in my life. It is a shame when adults fight and younger people get the brunt of our anger; shame on us. Shame on anyone who puts or uses a kid in the middle or dangles them as a carrot to win a fight. In the end, the one who puts the child in the middle will have to deal with that guilt. The parent's or elder's faults become the child's burden, and who are we to place a burden on the innocent?

Mom and I became friends due to the fact that she offered healing to me. Over time, I forgave my anger toward my mom. I did not want her to go to bed feeling like she had failed. We have humbled ourselves before one another and before God. We have asked for forgiveness and we have healing. We can get mad at one another, but who cares anymore? It is anger, so what? It will burn off after a walk around the block. It can make for great reality TV. Again,

Journey of the Son

so what. We love each other; that is what matters and we know it. Nothing else does. When something else matters, we have a road block and the relationship is not experiencing truth. When truth is hindered, get ready for tension, sleepless nights, anger, resentment, a feeling of entitlement, and so on.

I would get on my knees and pray to God: "God, what is love? I want to know what love is."

1 Corinthians 13

If I speak in the tongues of men or of angels, but do not have love, I am only a resounding gong or a clanging cymbal. If I have the gift of prophecy and can fathom all mysteries and all knowledge, and if I have a faith that can move mountains, but do not have love, I am nothing. If I give all I possess to the poor and give over my body to hardship that I may boast, but do not have love, I gain nothing. Love is patient, love is kind. It does not envy, it does not boast, it is not proud. It does not dishonor others, it is not self-seeking, it is not easily angered, it keeps no record of wrongs. Love does not delight in evil but rejoices with the truth. It always protects, always trusts, always hopes, always perseveres. Love never fails. But where there are prophecies, they will cease; where there are tongues, they will be stilled; where there is knowledge, it will pass away. For we know in part and we prophesy in part, but when completeness comes, what is in part disappears……..

And now these three remain: faith, hope and love. But the greatest of these is love."

Do I know hope? Yes I do. DO I know faith? Faith in what? God? Yes I have faith that a being, not human, created this universe. I do have faith in that. Do I know love? It is the greatest; wouldn't I want to know the greatest? Yes I do want to know it and I do know love to the extent that I have allowed myself the experience. At times in my life I have experienced love to the point that I am overwhelmed. At times in my life, I have been without, I was filled with myself and I was empty. No matter where I was in my life, these verses have always been in my mind. I really focused on the fact there are three—faith, hope and love--but only one is the greatest. This chapter tells me I can have all the knowledge in the world and if I have not love, I have nothing.

Chapter 5

TRACK IS MY SANCTUARY

Have you ever been gripped with fear? I have. Once abuse sets in, security is taken away. With this being said, I have noticed through my years of training children that when a child is not disciplined, you had best watch out because bad things are going to happen. Spanking and abuse are different. There are ground rules and children must know that when he/she walks over the line, there will be discipline. Whatever form that may be. I'm not telling you how to discipline your kid, but I am telling you to be the parent and let the child know he/she is not to walk all over you. Sometimes it can be done with humor, a talk, or a hug. There are times when a belt to the backside is the only alternative.

I was 9 when my father lost his temper and first struck me. There were many times that I needed to be disciplined as a child, but when a child is hit out of anger or rage it is a different ball game entirely. He never hit me again like that until I was around 12. Once it started, he kept doing it. He called it discipline. It was not.

When you discipline a child, there are specific consequences for specific actions: three licks for back talking, no allowance if chores are not completed, and a docked allowance if the parent has to ask more than three times for something. Get it?

My discipline consisted of my father swinging the thick leather weightlifting belt he used, an action which ended when his face lost its redness and his anger burnt off. If he got real pissed, I got the buckle end.

What is scary, or what was for me about living with an abuser, was that I never knew what was going to set the abuser off. Yes, we all make mistakes, but the abuser gets to decide how pissed he or she is going to get and how much hell he or she is going to inflict on the home. What a coward the abuser is! The abuser takes advantage of the weak, the ones who love him or her; they drag people into their own personal hell. As a child, I thought, "Where is my protector in this world?" Under these circumstances, there is no such thing as firm

Journey of the Son

footing in your home life. When this happens, where do you get your footing?

For me, it first and for a long time, became the track. There is nothing like an empty track, being able to go there and feel the wind brushing past my ears, pushing my body and learning to control my breath, heart rate, and thoughts as I push through an interval workout on the track or the challenging one lap all-out test. I usually save that for my birthday – this is my answer to staving off Father Time. The track became my sanctuary – even though it was located in the outdoors! Not only was it my safe haven, it was also the place I felt most connected with God.

LOVE IN ACTION

I at least do know what love is from my father. My father spent a lot of time with me as a young boy. Every weekend visit, he would take me running or hit tennis balls with me. It takes love to spend the time. That also helped to instill the discipline part of my life which my dad taught me by his actions. He did this well, and it has greatly benefitted my life. No matter how bad I cried or complained that I hurt, Dad made me finish the 3-mile run every weekend.

He was right there by my side. "Come on, son. You can make it. Breathe it out." He took me to my first track meets. He would stand there at the end of the 100m finish line and tell me to run, to keep on running until I hit his arms. My father was there to catch me and protect me. I was 5 when I ran my first track meet. He hugged me; he would give me kisses all over my face. I knew my dad loved me. There was no doubt in this early assurance.

I know what it is like to have a father who will protect me. I was a brave, brave child in many ways. That is why I felt as if the carpet got yanked out from under my feet when my teen years began to arrive. My protector was gone. He turned against me – and others. I needed protection from him, and I got scared – really scared. This was reflected in my life outside of the house. I stopped sticking up for myself and I let people run over me. I stopped fighting for my wants outside of the typical teenage desires. This is why I became so angry at God as well. How could my dad change like this? Where is the man who raised me? Where is my security, God!?

Journey of the Son

CHOICES

My father more than anything else wanted family. He wanted to be loved. I just don't think he was willing to pay the price of self-sacrifice for a family. In a family, we cannot always take care of ourselves and when you are the head of the household you get the brunt of a lot of the burden. Let's get real – it can be a very thankless job. In sports, we have a phrase we use when we talk about leaders, those who are "first to arrive and last to leave." This is what leaders do. They deflect the credit and accept the blame, even if it isn't their fault. This is what the head of a family will do. That person will take care of the problems in house. You never expose your family, your team, to embarrassment and humiliation. Dad did this to me a lot. He embarrassed those around him if they messed up.

I know my father knows how to love. Just like Luke Skywalker, he believed there was good in his father, Darth Vader. He could feel it. It was hidden behind a mask but he could feel there was good. He just knew it. I had assurance due to my younger days that my dad who raised me from my younger years still existed within him.

Thirteen days after my father's suicide attempt, he could not speak. He had a stroke. I will never forget that day. He was recovering just fine, and then there was silence. Nothing. He was just lying there in the hospital bed; this was the first time in my life that I felt old. I was 35. I had such hope dad would be up and at 'em once he got released from intensive care and it was looking that way. From day 6 to day 12 things were going great. He was recovering just fine and looked strong. Then, the dark night of the soul set in.

Many months went by before he could speak again. From day 6 to day 12 of his recovery he could speak and I was able to hear things that I had not heard out of his mouth in a long, long time: thankfulness and love. All of these types of words came from his mouth. Then the silence started.

One of my most nerve-wracking moments was when he gained his speech back. What was he going to say? Initially (day 6 to day 12) I heard loving and kind words, but so did I when I was a child. The same person spoke awfully to me later on in my life. It was hard for me to believe what I heard just a few months earlier was what I would hear again now that he had

Journey of the Son

gained his speech back. "I love you, son," is what I heard – words we all are dying to hear from our father: "I love you." He thanked me for being his son. The goodness in his heart came out through his words. Some of us are so stubborn that we need something for us to realize and verbalize what matters most to us.

Some of us are also stubborn in believing others. I do agree that in a moment a life can change. A belief system can be altered inside of a moment. There are also those of us who are damaged and it will take repetitious behavior for us to finally believe the new paradigm. Unfortunately in this case, I am one who needs to hear how I am appreciated, at least from my father. It has taken me a long time to be 100% comfortable in my own skin. Will I be accepted for who I am? My father couldn't, so it seemed. And here lies the lie: He couldn't accept himself, and for one to love another they must first know how to have love for themselves. The lie kept me from believing that I was worthy of being accepted and loved for many years.

What a parent can do to a child will either catapult them into greatness in their adult life or leave them much baggage to deal with. I have had to carry this baggage with me most of my life. I stopped my life so I could "straighten things" up. I am okay. I am dealing with it just fine. I have implemented steps to recognize when I am falling into my traps. It can be hard to deal with, when these traps "rear their heads" in my life, but I am making it just fine. As with anything it takes time for a new behavior to become habit. Once it does become habit, the life we seek can accelerate at immense speeds. This is the quantum jump I referred to in the sprint race of life. We hit the turbo button and speed on in the race of life.

For those who can identify with me, say it in your head, and say it out loud: I AM LOVED. Say it 10 times, then smile real big. It makes me laugh when I say it, and laughing helps my heart smile. Don't you feel better!?

Chapter 6

Burning Questions

Writing a book can unveil a lot of things you never knew were in you, things you forgot about. I can recall the moment I was first exposed to that other side of my father:

I never knew what it was like for my parents to be under the same roof. As I alluded, I only saw them fight and have disdain for one another. There was this a particular weekend when my father came to pick me up. For some reason, I wanted my mom. I just didn't want to leave the house. Mom, standing behind a locked door, told my dad I didn't want to go. He started beating on the door. I could just hear this voice and this banging on the door, pounding on the door. I saw the door rattling, as he was kicking on it. This scared the hell out of me. This is the first time I saw this side of my father. There was a side of me recognizing that if he could lose it like this toward my mother then he could also lose it like this on me. I was 5. Mom called the police. I could hear his voice: "Let me see my son! Let me see my son!" Memories like this are embedded deep within.

I must have felt bad, thinking I was also responsible for my father acting out. Was it directed at me? Talk about abandonment for my dad – he loves his son and his son doesn't want to see him. That has to be hard. I wonder if every time something like this happened in his life if all his scars from his father's relationship would come rushing to the surface.

The movie *Field of Dreams* would provoke a reaction from my father. My dad has a memory of his father coming out to the side yard to play catch with him as a young boy. My dad threw the ball hard, trying to impress his father and when it hit the mitt, the ball hurt his hand. His dad was a bocce player and grew up playing soccer. His dad threw down the mitt, rubbed his hand, and never played baseball with my father again. The movie *Field of Dreams* revolves around a father-son relationship. The son needed to build a baseball diamond in his corn field so his father could return from the afterlife

Journey of the Son

to have one more game of catch with him.

I knew what the movie was about. For us, it is about the absence of a father-son relationship. It is the attempt at healing that relationship. The movie is about saying the things you should have said or wanted to do but never did with that person. After watching the movie one night, I asked my father a question concerning the topic of this movie. My father replied to me behind many tears, "I don't know, he would never play catch with me again." The pivotal scene of the movie was the father and son having a game of catch – just like with my father and his father. The main character was played by Kevin Costner and my dad felt connected with him because they had something in common: they both wanted to have one last game of catch with their respective dads. Here lies the rejection of my father from his father. Forever he has asked himself if he did something wrong. If only he wouldn't have wanted to impress his father and if he hadn't have thrown so hard, maybe his dad would have wanted to play with him again – or so he at least thought. "Why did my father reject me?" This is the burning question my father has wanted an answer to all of his life. It's a question I have as well. My father passed that on to me. He never settled on a satisfactory answer in his own heart and he passed his turmoil on to my generation, to me.

I'll never forget the last scene: Kevin Costner's father, who was a young man in this scene, looked at his son and asked, "Is this heaven?" The son looked at his dad, "No, it's Iowa." The way they said the lines, the viewer knew they both knew who they were talking to. In so few words they said to each other, "Forgive me. I love you." The father was able to say to the son, "I'm sorry for putting the pressure on you. I'm sorry for being stubborn. I'm sorry for not reaching out to you in a way you could understand." The son was able to say to the father, "I'm sorry for being so judgmental, for not forgiving you. For not speaking with you once I became a man and left home." This is what my father needed and wanted to hear from his father so badly.

The burning question my dad wanted an answer to was the same burning question I wanted an answer to. I wanted to know: Where did you go, dad? You were there for me as a child; why have you disappeared?

I knew dad needed absolution from the same questions centering on this movie. The little boy in him spoke out from a 45-year-old body. I do believe that my dad finally got peace. He had to have peace in order to move on. He couldn't leave this life until he attained peace with knowing how to accept love.

Dysfunction Invites Co-dependency

Due to my need for approval and the dysfunctional relationships at home, I found myself gravitating toward co-dependent relationships. I picked the wrong type of women to be around. I looked for relationships to give me something that they couldn't. I looked for my successes at work and for certain individuals to fill the void in my life. This was unfair and put immense pressure on an individual or circumstance. In the end, this behavior is not healthy and it led me away from taking real looks at myself. Dysfunctional relationships are not love relationships. Is there love somewhere in there? Most of the time, the dysfunction smothers the love. The dysfunction sucks the oxygen out of the room and all a person wants is out of the room so they can breathe. Have you ever met a person and 90 % of them is absolutely great, but the 10 % that is bad about them eliminates the 90 % that is good about them? This would be a red flag letting you know there is some type of severe dysfunction in their life.

Have you ever been in a relationship and it was just bad, bad, bad? Was no one around you (friends and family) telling you to keep on with the relationship? Or, as I have heard one person call it, a "relationshit."

In short, I think the reason why I have been so drawn to dysfunctional relationships and have dealt with co-dependent relationships is because of what I was born into. My mother and father were set for divorce. Mom became pregnant and they delayed the divorce. Eight months into my life, my parents finally ended their misery with each other and divorced. They decided to go on and achieve misery away from one another. I say misery because until change happened inside of their own thinking, they repeated the cycle again, which my father did later on in his second marriage.

My mother and father's relationship was dysfunctional. There was abuse, co-dependency, and I think both of them were addicted to sex – hence, I came into existence. Thank God, I was not aborted. Mom wanted out of the home life she had grown up in; she wanted out of the

Journey of the Son

home in which she was abused, but she traded one abusive home for another.

Dad and mom had that "fatal attraction" thing going on. Both of their deficiencies in life drew them to each other. This is a great example of what a "relationshit" is. One's deficiencies call out to another, and for some reason you are lethally attracted to one another. I have experienced enough "black widows" in my life. It is to my great advantage to run from these types of women. For most of my life, I attracted these women like white does to rice. Why do I attract them? I have grown up in this environment in which I am tuned in to fatal attracters. I give off those vibes – at least I used to. I have changed and do not tolerate the red flags. I have no desire to "fix" another person anymore.

Another factor as to why I fight for love is that I had to fight for my love from Mom. Eventually this same thing happened with my father as well. I think the right way to say it is Mom had to fight to be loved and as a result, had a difficult time giving love to others. There is a notion many therapists have used that says "one must know love in order to be able to love." That can perhaps describe her. Mom was stripped of many things when she was sexually abused as a child – love being one of them. She was stripped of knowing how to trust love, let herself be loved, and how to love others. The walls of protection were high and thick with her. This is something she has to be very conscious of every day of her life. The violation against her makes her prone to a stance of protection. This platform of thinking tricks you into someone or something is always looking to take from you. She stays on guard at all times. It is hard for mom to relax and be at peace. Why? Because someone took her innocence, took her security as a child. She's standing guard to make sure no one violates her ever again. Even what most see as the smallest event to her, triggers the original violation.

Dysfunctional people usually attract the dysfunctional aspects out of the people in their lives. It is a constant cycle any addict goes through. You don't have to be addicted to alcohol or drugs to be called an addict. There are a lot of people out there who are addicted to the approval of others. Usually this is a byproduct of some other deficiency in one's life.

So, when I was a teenager, my world really

Journey of the Son

got turned upside down. My mother remarried and I moved in with my father. I refused to live with my mother after she got married. I didn't want to be under the same roof with the man she was marrying. He didn't want to be under the same roof with me either. We agreed on that.

Dad and I were definitely bachelors. Anything went on in his house. Actually, my friends (Spicer, Marty, Tommy, Christian, and Argo) and I started a fraternity house and guess whose house was the headquarters? That's right! Dad actually helped us get the whole thing up and running. We had a credo, officer titles, etc. We could do anything in that house, and then it all went to hell in a hand basket.

Dad got himself a girlfriend! That sucked big time. She didn't like dad and me burping at the dinner table. Farting was eliminated as well. We had to chew food with our mouths closed. It was a bummer for me and my "fraternity brothers." Before this woman, dad had a healthy distance between himself and his "lady friends." He let this one get all into in his business. This was foreign territory for me.

I was resistant to the relationship just as I was with my mother's relationship. The now stepparents didn't want to deal with me. I don't blame them. I began to feel as if I was a byproduct of a relationship that did not exist anymore and somewhat felt as if my parents wished there was not any evidence of the relationship. That is how I felt as a teenager. Today I know that I have made mistakes in relationships. I used to rid myself of any evidence of those relationships. The result: I understand by way-of-life experience what my father and mother were going through a little bit better. I have lived out some of their mistakes.

Today, this "enlightenment phase" has allowed me to have a lady friend and she is the best lady friend I have been involved with. Aren't you laughing? I am still so demented about relationships that I cannot even go to "that place" about any kind of "girlfriend" talk. Fortunately, She is really cool.

I have become involved in a 12-step program which allowed me to further my understanding of what is right and wrong inside of a relationship between individuals, whether it be a friendship, committed relationship, lady friend, or a family relationship. Knowledge of right and wrong actions within a relationship allows for health between people.

One more thing about relationships: I realized somewhere in my late 20's that I did not have to be married. That was a freedom that helped me greatly. I didn't NEED someone. I DIDN'T HAVE to get married. I grew up in the Bible Belt which is located in the Southern United States. We are typically told and grown to be married by the mid-twenties. There is nothing wrong with being married – it all comes down to why we are getting married. At least to me, the "why" is very important. I think in the 20's there is all this excitement about "I'm going to get married" scenario. It's their day and so it should be.

I think a freedom from the obligation of marriage allowed me to do what or where I felt I was being directed in my life. I had certain itches I wanted to scratch, goals I had to accomplish and I didn't know how to accomplish them while dealing with the emotions of another person. I didn't know she should be responsible for her emotions. I felt too greatly for those I let in to my heart. If they are to have a meltdown, it was hard to have that tug on me. I couldn't afford to give enough of myself in a romantic relationship to sacrifice my goals in life.

Then in my 30's when some of those goals were being laid to rest, I realized something else: intense hate residing in my soul. Intense hate directed toward my father. It got to the point where this hate was interfering with my everyday life because it was affecting my thought life. I remember a conversation with my mother: I was standing outside of a track stadium. I was so distraught, so angry. I told her: "That's it, Mother: I have to stop this. I feel cursed. I have never seen anyone with a happy marriage in all my life. I can't seem to find love in my own life. If I am to never marry, to never have children so this generational curse can be stopped then so be it."

I did want to be loved and I wanted to love someone in a boyfriend-girlfriend relationship. I didn't want to drag her through my personal hell. I realized if I wanted this, then I had to fix my relationship with my father before I attempted a relationship with a woman once again. I eat one food group at a time when I eat. I don't mix. I eat one group then move on to the next. This is how I was dealing with my relationships as well. I needed to deal with my father before I went on to my "sweet potatoes."

I began this healing part of my journey by

simply picking up a phone. I called my father; I had to for my own good.

If I were to ever be married, I was going to be asking her to marry more than me. I would be asking her to join my family. I wanted to bring her into some sort of happiness. I didn't want any woman to be with me or start a home with me if I wasn't whole. It has taken me a long time to plug my holes. I think this book has forced me to find the deepest cracks and then find a way to fill my holes with answers I could live with. I am in my 40's today and maybe, just maybe I could be in a place where I could marry if I choose to do so. I'm not all the way there in some areas but emotionally I would say I am at a point where it is possible.

Chapter 7

THE POINT OF THE GREAT DIVIDE

In my teen years, as I lived with dad and the girlfriend thing was happening, dad started to become abusive. Even more so, after a period of time, I started to see him become very abusive to his girlfriend who then became his wife. She got it worse than I did. I confess that I didn't feel sorry for her. She knew how to push his buttons and wouldn't let off of the gas pedal. He would ask her to give it a rest and she wouldn't let the nagging and badgering go. She got her hooks into him and it messed with his head. Once again, there was another dysfunctional relationship for him.

As I look back at dad, his abuse heightened a great deal after he met this woman. This is the perfect example of two people who should have never gotten married. Once he started to hit her, she should have walked out the door. Once he realized that this woman was not going to listen to him, but instead nag and provoke him to an emotional state in which he became a menace to society, he should have walked his ass out of the door as well. Dad, why didn't you walk out that door!?

Do I condone the abuse? No. Women are not innocent, either. There are many out there, and I call them black widows. They eat their man. That is what the spider does – the female eats the male widow after they mate. Due to my dysfunctions, I could attract some really "good" ones. I have been eaten or have been attempted to be eaten a few times. Luckily, I was not an asshole, but when I got pushed to a point – all that fight in me got pointed at them. Fortunately, I can say I have never hit a woman.

In the movie, *Princess Bride* there is a scene in which the battle of wits takes place. Death is on the line! Some of my "battle of wits" felt like death was on the line. I could feel these women trying to take my soul from me. I have made it out of these relationships. Any time one goes in for a fight there are some types of wounds to deal with. There is always some ramification. I am alive and my heart is still alive today. I have to do certain things to fight for it, and it still beats today.

Due to these battles with black widows, I have developed what I call a "spider sense." My insides start tingling when I come across a black widow. I have the curiosity of a cat and hopefully nine lives. I'm about on life number 30 in this area.

During his marriage, my dad was changing and the love I knew with my father as a child was leaving the building, like Elvis. Now, I was living with someone that could spin into a rage at any second. One was fire and the other was gasoline. The fire was already lit; she felt the need to pour the gasoline on him.

Just because I was developing into an adult didn't mean that I didn't need love. I wanted to hear words of love from the man who would tell me all the time as a child. I started to figure out that I would receive love when I did something good, when I performed. Meanwhile, I still had this resentment growing in me toward my dad at this point. I resented him for pulling the plug on our relationship. I resented him for turning his back on me. I think I did hate him for hitting me. I feel as though this plays a big part as to how I treat people I commit to today. When I commit to a person, I will walk to the ends of the earth to give them every opportunity to succeed.

The Darkest Hours

This is as dark as it got for me inside Albert's home. We all lived in fear. Eventually. someone has to give in. Why did I always have to fight for every inch with my dad? I began to fight everyone in my home and everything my home represented – including God.

I eventually got to the end of my rope, at least for this particular season in my life. Dad would read the Bible to us at night. He would gather us all in a room and read, as a family. HE thought we were happy and this was what HE was SUPPOSED to be doing. "This is what Christian leaders do." Eyes would often roll in response.

It is funny; none of us kids were buying into the program—not me or my two young stepsisters. I think if kids are not buying into it, maybe the adults taking part should ask themselves if they are being truthful with themselves. Kids are great at picking up on BS. My dad was trying to do what he thought he was supposed to do. The church tells you to be

Journey of the Son

the spiritual leader of the household. Deep down, I am not sure how much he believed in it himself. We kids were being force-fed the Bible by a man who beats his wife. We got abused as well. We lived in fear of the tyrant. It wasn't a secure home. The tyrant of the household was preaching God's love to us. As much love as he would show, we also had that much fear and more. It didn't seem to even out. We learned to prepare for the worst. The pain of his worst hurt a lot more than a pleasure of joy from the love we felt.

I have realized that it wasn't the Bible I refused to listen to, rather, it was my dad whom I wasn't listening to.

I would lie in bed at night and pray to God that I would not believe in God. Oxymoron there – I was praying to God that I would STOP believing in him. It was built in me, knowing there is a God/Creator, and I couldn't deny it.

As my father would read to us, I would purposefully and intentionally shut his words out. I was mad at God. I was mad about being in that house and mad at my father who raised me and abandoned me. He was there, but it wasn't the same man. I know there are those of you out there who hate hearing about the Bible, hate hearing the word "God."

You know what I want to tell you? Rock on! There is a strong chance what you are rejecting is not the Bible. It is not God you are rejecting, but the source it is coming from. You may even be closer to having faith than the one who is at church every Sunday and Wednesday evening out of mere routine. You are rejecting religion being stuffed down your throat and you are just like I was at 15 when my father would read the Bible to me. It was not the Bible, God's word, I was rejecting. It was the source it was coming from. He couldn't live his life in a manner worthy of respect and as a result, I did not believe in anything coming from his mouth.

Life was turning me into a student: Believe peoples' actions, not their words.

Religion hides behind God's name in order to promote its own plan. Never use God's name to endorse your personal plans.

Eventually everything came to a halt. Another blow up/ blow out at the Santi household and I left and walked out the door. My dad, this time, called the police on me for leaving the house. I wouldn't come home and they couldn't find me. The police actually did find my location, though my cousin Robert had told them he had not seen me. Eventually, I did go home.

I laugh at how the police have been called on me – they have been called on me because I left the house and they have been called on me because I wouldn't leave the house. Damned if you do and damned if you don't. These are the only times ever in my life the police have been called on me. Dad used the police instead of parenting. He wouldn't get sex if his wife was pissed at me. He would ask himself, "What do I need to do?" She was in such control of him.

"I want Marc out of the house"… "son, get out."

"No, dad."

"You're not going to obey me in my own home… I'm going to call the police."

That is how the police would get called on me.

I returned home after this one blow up and I remember hearing that belt jingling. My dad was coming down the hall from his room to my room with the weightlifting belt. This was my wake up call for church that morning. A weightlifting belt is thick, very thick, and heavy leather. Dad woke me up and said, "Bend over." I was 17 at this point in my life. I was still undersized at this time (5'4" 120lbs). My dad was more along the lines of 5'9" and 190lbs. I bent over and he took to whooping my butt. He would hit and hit until his anger subsided.

I had enough. I stood upright and turned to look him in the face.

He looked at me and said, "Bend over. You will obey me in my house."

I looked him back in his eyes and I said to him, "No more! You're not going to hit me anymore."

My door was shut and locked. I realized Superman was not going to bust down the door and save me. The only person who was going to save me was ME.

He turned the belt to the other end and started to swing the buckle side facing me. He swung at my head and toward whatever he could hit. He was really losing it this time. I tucked down and put my fists up. I swung. I

Journey of the Son

feared if I hit him squarely in the face that he might kill me. I hit him in the stomach two quick times. He then started to wrestle me down to the ground. I wasn't going easily. He somehow got behind me and the next thing I saw was his arm coming around from my side and around my neck. He got me in a choke hold. His 190 pounds was riding my back as he was choking me. I fell to the ground and with all my might I was trying to get to my feet, to break free. My vision started to close in, and it was getting dark. The dark walls were closing in on me until all I could see was through a very small tunnel. The oxygen was being choked from me. I couldn't get any air. I thought that was it for me. I really thought my dad was going to kill me.

I tried to break free, and if I had, I was going for my baseball bat. I was going to kill him. I was going to do what I needed to do to protect myself. I didn't make it to my bat. He eventually released his grip. I laid there gasping for air. I don't know if I was in shock as to what had just happened. All I remember was that he got up, picked up that belt, and hit me again. I was too broken to hit back.

Well, that is how he chose to wake me for

church that morning. Dad went on to teach at his college and career class that day at a church where the head pastor was giving the old one-eye to his secretary. His secretary wasn't his wife either. What a fine example this church is to the business that church has become. Sign me up!

I shut down. I wouldn't speak with my father any more. I did not know this man. This was not the man who raised me. This grew into intense anger. My anger eventually turned inward and I did not care about living any more. Suicide was starting to become an option. The only thing keeping me from following through was what I consider the greatest gift God has ever blessed me with: a younger brother – Patrick.

Rising From The Ashes

Returning to the story at hand, one may ask: What did dad do by middle of "fight" week? He told me, "You are going to talk to a drug abuse counselor." It turned out that the counselor was tied into a long-term drug rehabilitation program that was tied into the church my dad was working for. Next thing I know I was being admitted into the program as a drug abuser.

Journey of the Son

People were in the program for two years. Meth heads, cocaine, heroin. You name it, they had done it. Here I was in drug rehab, clumped in with all these individuals. I was shaking my head with disbelief. I had to physically fight my father and now I had to mentally and emotionally fight off this. What else could be thrown at me?

Eventually, they did administer a drug test and psychological testing. Guess what the results indicated? Figuring that I had never come home drunk in my life and most of my friends thought I didn't drink, I was the designated driver for all my friends. I drove all their cars before I had my own car to drive. I drove their cars more than they drove their own cars.

After all the test results came back negative and 17 days had passed, the counselor then let us know this was not the place for us but we did have intense family problems. REALLY?! Who would have guessed that?

Then I was sent to another treatment facility. Off to the mental hospital for me! Happy, happy, joy, joy – off I go to the MENTAL HOSPITAL! Why? Because a volcano met a tornado and I have a knack for causing it to erupt – at least at this point in time. I could see the fault and I would pick at it. I had my way of judging and I was hard-headed. I was going to do my thing and I wasn't good at buying your Oscar Meyer bologna.

I was classified as a general psychiatric patient. There were also the CDs (chemical dependents), as they were in the other wing.

When you're there, you have a case worker, a personal doctor who meets with you, and your immediate family members in a private setting and then you have the group therapy with your family members along with about five to eight other patients and their families.

I didn't know what they wanted me to say. I was just being a teenage kid. I did what the program called for: going to my meetings during the day. Ironically, I had a great time while I was there. I found the humor in things. I had tons of fun with everyone. This is where I started to figure out that girls found me attractive. I ended up making friends with most of the girls there and I started to come out of my shell. By the end, I got their numbers. I really didn't know what to do with a woman/girl yet at this point in my life. All I knew to do was just be me, talk to them like I

Journey of the Son

would a friend. It is amazing what a woman/girl will share with you when you are a trusted friend.

There were a few volatile moments during my stay there concerning my therapy. All involved my father and me. We were in this private therapy session; it was my father, his wife, the doctor, and me. I knew insurance would only pay for 21 days. It was around day 14. The doctor said to me, "Marc, your dad and Connie feel as if you do not want to come home to them after your stay here is over."

I sat there and mulled it over it in my head. I knew this was another pivotal moment in my life. I thought, "If I lie and say 'yes' I will be home in 7 days, hanging out with my friends, playing baseball in the city league" (which I was the first pick in the draft). I looked at the doctor, and this is what a 17-year-old boy said to him, "You're damn right! I don't *ever* want to live with that man again." So, apparently the fight hadn't completely gone out of me yet. In the last month, I had the police called on me and had a fist fight with my father due to fact that he was beating the shit out of me. I have been accused of being on drugs and shipped off to long-term drug rehab. Now, I get to face the bully once more along with his new side kick (the doctor).

My father got on the edge of his seat and I swear on my life, I saw smoke come out of the top of his head. He was bright red. What little hair he had was standing straight up. He said, "That's it, if I can't have you, no one can have you. I am going to send you away, so far away. You're going to a survival wilderness camp and you are going to have to hunt in the woods for your food and if a bear gets you, so what." I really don't know what he said after that because I was freaked out. What I know is that I stood up once again. How many times am I going to have to stand up to this guy? The doctor looked at me like I had done something wrong. I stood up for myself and the doctor backed the abuser, the bully. Doc, you had a man in your office that beats the hell out of his wife and his son. He was in full anger/rage mode and you backed him. Way to go, Doc!

This scared me to death. I remember going to bed that night crying and shaking. I said to myself, "That is it. I am sick of all this fighting. I have tried and tried to do it my way and it is not working out." I was shaking in my bed, trembling with fear at what is to come. I was convinced my father was going to follow through. All the fear of my life came rushing back in.

I prayed the prayer, "Lord Jesus come into my heart as my Lord and Savior." A flood of peace came over me. It was like warm water ran through my soul and comforted me. I felt like Peter – when I looked to Jesus I was brave and had the faith to walk on water. When I looked at the waves, the wind, the rain, and took my eyes away from Jesus, I sank in the water. I began to tremble with fear as I lay in bed. That is how I came to know Jesus Christ as my personal Savior.

I always knew God's hand was on me from a young age. I grew up in a Christian home. This is how I was raised. I remember telling my mother I might want to be a priest at a very early age. She wasn't shocked. I meant it, too.

Days after I asked Christ into my heart, I still had hate in my heart. I tried to let it go. I had this anger within me, though it didn't always present itself as anger to others around me. I controlled it.

I found myself in another private therapy appointment – this time, with my mom, Aunt

Kathy, and the same doctor who earlier in the week was backing the "rage machine" of my father. This appointment was set up to be a healing therapy session between mom and me. Mom and I fought but we didn't hate one another. We were not at the root cause of our reasons for fighting. We just fought. We made life difficult on one another, but as iron sharpens iron. By the way – do you know what happens when two iron heads collide? Sparks fly and when they keep colliding, heat and friction occur. Eventually the iron heads melt together due to the heat. I have always heard the expression but never put any thought to it.

Mom and I collided and eventually we melted into one another. We stopped the resistance with one another. We love one another and started to realize we should probably stop being each other's punching bags. Aren't relationships between people funny? It is ironic how we need each other. We really do.

Mom was not at the root of my anger, my hate. My father was. In this session with this doctor, I couldn't find anything to work on with Mom. I couldn't get past my hate toward my father. I expressed so clearly how pissed off I was at him. I had tears of anger and hurt in my eyes. The doctor actually did his job well in this session. He told me, "I want you to write all this in a letter to your father (my feelings of hate and anger). You must read it to your father in the next family session/group therapy." Family session was where a psychologist, seven patients, and our immediate family gathered in a room for 90 minutes. We would discuss what we were working on in our therapy and how we progressed throughout the week.

I wrote my letter. I saved the letter for years. "Hello dad, I am writing this letter to let you know I hate you. Every time we go and play tennis I try to hit you with the tennis ball. I started lifting weights because one day, I am going to be bigger and stronger than you and you will know what it is like lying on the ground looking up at me and begging me to stop hitting you. You will know what it is like to live in fear of me..."

I wrote my letter and now I had to read it to his face. Yet again, I knew I have to do something I really don't want to do but I have to in order to set myself free. I had to face the bully again. I had to stand up to the man who has caused me to live in fear. It's worse than a bully at school. You can't go home and away from this bully. My bully was supposed to be my protector in life. Why God, WHY? I am just 17 years old. I live in the suburbs of America. Why do I have to do this? My teenage years are not supposed to unfold like this!

Oh, I sat in that group meeting and I desperately had thoughts as to why I should not read my letter. Ten minutes went by and there was a pause, an opportunity for someone to speak in the group. Long pause... I rose my hand to speak...I read my letter.

My father sat there with his wife and she spoke up for him and denied every bit of it. There I was 17 years old; I confronted him once more and I was about to have another adult walk out on me – AGAIN! I sat there and I started to cry as I said to my stepmother, "I am out on a limb here, do not leave me out here. We have a chance to stop this." She started to cry and she backed me. I think it is the best thing my stepmother did for me in the course of our time together. She backed me and we stood against the man who was beating us. He was responsible for our life of fear, at least while living inside of that household.

I don't know why and what attracted her to my father. It was one of "those" relationships for the lot of us who have come from abusive upbringings are well aware of. For some unknown reason, we were just drawn to it. It calls our name.

What ensued after the letter was the most explosive family session this doctor had ever been a part of. That was a direct quote from his mouth 11 years later. This was a completely different doctor than my personal doctor. The family session went well over time. It would be considered pinned-to-your-seat viewing if it was television. There was another father in the room and he let it be known he did not agree with what was going on in my father's household. He let it be known if you wanted to hit on someone come hit on me – not a kid and a woman. I wish I knew his name. I would thank him.

The session went to such a climax, the two men nearly stood up and met in the middle of the room. This session was an inch away from turning into Monday Night Wrestling. My dad would never relinquish. He would not admit to any wrongdoings. This other man was a big man. Both men wanted to take each other's heads off, and it almost happened. I swear, you could see both of them about to rip the arms off of their chairs as they were trying to hold themselves in them. They both wanted to pounce on one another.

After that, up and away I was sent.

Up Up and Away

Dad did just what he said he was going to do when he was in one of his intense anger modes; I got shipped off to a survival wilderness camp. Altogether, my experience lasted eight months.

I can remember riding to the airport with mom. I was glad to see her and ride with her. I still could care less about seeing my father and riding with him. He was the enemy in my mind. Mom brought some peace to the situation. She told me this would be good for me. I was a little bit shocked by the whole thing, but somehow, someway, I let God hold my hand and guide me through. I was scared. We have all had those moments in life we do not want to live out. The moments we want to shut our eyes and hope that when we open them that it will all be better. When I opened my eyes, the moment was still there. I was questioning if I could make it through. I learned I could move forward through this experience. Life by the inch is a

Journey of the Son

cinch; life by the yard is hard. One step at a time is what I was learning.

Then, there was the plane ride to Indianapolis.

I was greeted by my driver, Mark. He took me to the school in Indiana I would be attending until departure for Canada, where the survival wilderness camp was located – which would occur in about a month's time.

I was taken into the old school...kind of like the school in the movie *Hoosiers*. It was old. It had a basketball gym just like the school in Hoosiers. I love basketball, so was good with it. I was taken in to the office and Steve greeted me. He was a good guy. I liked him. I just remember sitting there in his office and I just started to cry after a while. I was answering his questions and he was a kind and understanding soul. I just couldn't believe I was there. I told him that, too. This is what my life had come to. Seventeen, the relationship with my father, bad home in my teen years, and now I felt like the carpet had been yanked from underneath me once more. It was a common theme in my life – the carpet getting yanked out from underneath me by my parents. This came to be my expectation.

Some kids were court-ordered there. Some were in the custody of the state and hence owned by the school. Some, just like me, were sent there by their parents. Some of the students were world-class screw ups. Some were hardened criminals. A lot of them died young. Drugs, crime, and jail followed a lot of the former students. They are lost souls this world has forgotten about.

The survival wilderness program in Canada was part of the summer curriculum. I became established there in Marion, Indiana. Things were going well for me. Of course, athletics helped me get noticed. I was able to establish the new mantle of "fastest kid in the house." There was a counselor, Waymon, who was blazing fast and the kids wanted to race him before we went to the gymnasium to play basketball. I asked if I could get in on the race as well. About 30 yards into the race, it was Waymon and I. Neck and neck, he barely edged me. Keep in mind, I am still this little skinny kid (5'6" 125 lbs). The guys in the house were amazed at my speed. And of course we go play basketball, and yes, I was good at that too. I would just like to reiterate, if you want to be an athlete, "speed kills." You can't guard or tackle what you cannot catch.

Journey of the Son

Something happened to me that would affect the rest of my life. A few days after establishing myself as the athlete of the house, I got injured.

The gymnasium at Marion Indiana was old. I was 5'7" at the time and I had wanted to dunk a basketball all my life. This was crucial for me – that I dunk a basketball on a 10-foot goal. I could dunk a tennis ball at this point in my life. I was 17, but a shorty at this time. The basketball goal was mounted a few feet out from the wall of this shoe box of a gymnasium. Some of the students were running and jumping off of the wall which would propel them way above the 10-foot basket so that they could throw the basketball down the hole. I am a purist; when I dunk I want it to be the real thing. It was so tempting to get to know how this felt. So, I attempted to jump off of the wall and propel myself up so I could throw the ball down the hole. One thing I will tell you about a Marcus Santi dunk – I don't throw a ball in the hole. I want to RIP the DAMN RIM OFF THE GOAL! That is what I want to do with the ball when I go into a dunk mode. I am looking to take your hand off if you dare put it in front of me and the rim of that goal.

Marcus Santi

I have a track background so I went at the wall with a high jump approach and planted my foot into the wall. It got stuck in that wall as I pushed against it. Needless to say, when I expected to go up I just folded into the wall. I fell to the ground. My knee was not in the same place as when I left the ground. I could feel it out of place, but I thought I could rub it and possibly walk it off. I could feel my knee sliding back into place and then heard this pop as it slid back into place. I don't know what normal is, but my knee corrected itself. It was out of place and then my ligaments put it back into place again. I am not sure exactly what happened.

I have broken my nose a few times while playing sports, twisted an ankle, etc., but I had never truly injured myself. Well, I truly injured myself this time – my knee. A severe injury and I could not walk. I was on crutches and my knee was so swollen that I could not see my knee cap for a week. I was not able to see an orthopedic doctor; they took me to a pediatrician in a small town in Indiana. He looked at it, gave me some anti-inflammatory pills, put me in a knee immobilizer and gave me crutches. That was about three days after the incident. I had no ice for my knee because the ice maker was broken.

Journey of the Son

When I look back on this, I see the blessing. If they would have taken me to an orthopedic doctor I would have never gone to Canada. I tore a ligament. I found that out much later, well after the trip to Canada was over. I would have been sent home, gotten surgery, and still been trapped in the hell hole I called home.

The other blessing: my strength was taken from me. I now had to relearn how to succeed. I didn't have my speed and my athleticism to rely on. I was 17, far from home, sent away, and in some way, there was a touch of rejection that I felt. An experience like this teaches one how to stand on one's own two feet. God lit a path for me to stand on my two feet and allowed me to feel his protection. It was good; things were okay. This was what I needed to do to become the man God and my destiny was designing me to be. I learned how to win without my strength. I was taken from all things I was familiar with. I was taken from my family, friends, home, and now, my athleticism was taken from me.

Thinking back, I know some of my more memorable moments in sports came through much adversity. I made the finals of a tennis tournament with a sprained ankle. About to retire in the first set of my first-round match, as I was walking up to the net to default, I got pissed and said to myself "no way." I was down 4-1 and I couldn't move. I dug deep and found a strategy that allowed me to win in two sets. I played again that night. Once again, I implemented the same strategy and won again in straight sets. That kid was irate; I beat him on one leg. These opponents were guys that I had .500 records against. Actually, I had a losing record against the second guy, but not that night.

I found strengths I never knew I had. In both instances, I never would have found this truth if I had not been hurt/injured. In Indiana, I found my personality. I discovered how to deal with things by intellectually dealing with situations with reasoning and emotional development. I couldn't escape by going for a run or allowing my faults to be looked over because I could skirt by on athletic success. I just had me, my crutches, a swollen knee and a knee immobilizer…oh yeah, and my personality. For those who know me, they don't know what I am better at – athletics or clowning around.

I learned to overcome. A counselor took my

walking cane and smashed it into a million pieces. I wouldn't say it was the kindest way to do something, but there is a side of me that liked what he did. He basically told me with his actions, "Stop being a weenie and start walking as if you don't have an injury." This was while I was in Canada. I started to do just that. Over the course of the next 12 weeks, I grew physically, emotionally, and mentally. At the end of the camp they gave out awards. I received honorable mention for the hardest working male camper. I gained over 20 pounds during that time. I would lift logs that people could not believe a guy my size could lift. I also received one more award. Every year, there is a squad in which nine people from the whole camp are inducted. This includes camp counselors, campers (male and female) – everyone including the black flies and mosquitoes are eligible. (Anyone who has been to Canada knows their official bird is the mosquito. They have eyes with pupils you can see.) Each person is inducted for a specific attribute – mine was growth. My name was put on a plaque with the other eight Eagle Squad members.

Canada changed me for the better. I learned how to overcome an injury. I learned how to develop the other areas of my life. I learned to trust others and I became more balanced.

Well, what do I have at this point? I still had plenty. I was blind to all of the assets I possessed. Most importantly, I had a new life. I had a better understanding of God and who/what he was. I love what Jim Valvano said as he received his last award at the ESPYs: "Cancer can take away all of my physical abilities. It cannot touch my mind, it cannot touch my heart, and it cannot touch my soul." To me, this says you can take swings at my exterior body, but you cannot touch my interior body. This is exactly what was going on with me. I was being tested with the fire life can throw at you. I was being reconstructed in a whole new way. It was my soul that was being rebuilt. It was my heart's mind, my heart's eyes, my heart's ears that were being rebuilt.

God taught me that it is the inside that makes me strong. "The LORD does not look at the things man looks at. Man looks at the outward appearance, but the LORD looks at the heart" (1 Samuel 16:7). If I look with my heart's eyes then I see the inside of a person. I see their heart. I see their true strength.

There are many of us who have great exteriors but not such good hearts. We use the power of our exterior to gain selfish desires. Does that leave us fulfilled?

All of us out there come from different backgrounds, races, and genders. We all have one thing in common – hearts. My heart is the same color as your heart.

Chapter 8

The Choice: Darth Vader vs Luke Skywalker:

Some of us turn into what we despise. People want justice. I wanted justice with my father. I swore justice. I swore it to myself and to my father's face in the letter I wrote to him. Nine years had passed since I read him the letter. I am 26. I am a man now. I have a man's body.

My opportunity came knocking. Dad came to my house looking for a fight. He was picking with his words. He goaded me. He had been drinking. His second wife was divorcing him. He was alone. I wouldn't give him his keys to drive home. He was telling me how he "could take me." I had my chance. I could have taken advantage of the situation with an opening to knock his block off. I knew I had the situation. I had laid awake in bed thinking of for so many years. It was here.

I was either going to become Darth Vader and give into my hate, or become strong and fight for the good in myself – become Luke Skywalker. I was tempted with the power of what it would feel like to strike down the abuser. I would only take his place, just like Luke Skywalker would have done if he would have struck his father down. Luke Skywalker risked his life to save his father. I didn't risk my life but I did save my own life.

I hugged him, took him in the house, and put him to bed. I would become just like him if I hit him. I didn't want his life. I have never wanted his life. I want my own life. I needed to stop what his father did to him and what he did to me. NO MORE to our family curse! My grandmother's kind heart that was passed onward to me won that night.

I gave myself the greatest gift I could have possibly given myself: forgiveness, and with that I gave myself FREEDOM from this curse that has followed the men of my family.

It is hard to work through the anger and hate to get to the point where you can stand up for yourself and do this with actions of love.

Journey of the Son

Believe in the good of yourself and not the lies the abuser raised you to believe. I believed in the good that the women of my family (grandma and Aunt Dodie) believed existed within me. Their love made me a better person. It always has.

Light must come out of darkness. We will demand it as people. There is only so much we will tolerate. I craved the light more than my hate. It was time for something different. I was sick of dealing with all the difficulties my hate was placing on me. The light had its voice. The darkness ran hiding like a vampire does from the light.

Regarding adult relationships, I would like to take a sidebar worth noting. When my mother met a new love in her life, she willingly dropped me off and exited my life to pursue her own. I do not now blame my mother nor do I have anger to her. Even though I was told to my face by her at that time: "Marc, I am moving on with my life…."

I remember as she told me this, she kept referring to me and Carl (new husband) dividing her. I did that to a degree, I admit, in fighting to keep my mom my mom. I didn't want to share her with Carl. I made it difficult for the man and I thought I hated him. It turns out that I didn't. My family would tend to fight non-stop. We did laugh and had our crazy moments, fun crazy moments, but we have left ourselves with a lot of baggage to deal with. I know my mother to this day has extreme guilt over this. I don't desire for her to have this guilt.

Back when I was 10, my mom had told me she was moving on. A part of me did feel she was blaming me for her turmoil. There was a part of myself that was left behind in that moment. My mother didn't and wouldn't do anything once the abuse began with my dad. This made me feel very alone. It is one thing to be lonely and it is another to know there is no one out there who I can run to in time of need. This caused a feeling of indifference. This is how I dealt with my situation. I developed this split inside so I could deal with life.

I had an indifference at times with my mom. With my father, I had the trauma of fighting for my life. I fought the man who was supposed to be my protector. I had to in order for me to have a say in this world. As I had alluded to, I went from feeling like he was Superman as a young boy to feeling as if he was on this planet to take me out by late boyhood.

Journey of the Son

As a result of my relationship with my mother and this heartbreak, I sought out women who almost exercised a spell over me. They could easily seduce me and I sought to "fix" them because what I was really seeking is healing of the broken heart I experienced with my mother. Women can take your heart and step all over it if we allow them too.

I do love women and want to feel their love. I have never fully trusted them or their love. This goes back to the moment where Mom told me she was moving on and I knew I wasn't allowed to come.

Every time I fall in love, or what I thought love was, I visit my pain. I have never known just how to fall in love with the right woman. I went to church to ask how to do this. I had to leave the organized religion and for a time, I did put my Bible down. I had to find a way to relearn about love. Even as I have relearned, setting new patterns is hard and it is hard for old grooves to simply go away.

I believe memories can embed themselves into the cells of our bodies. The heartbreak I experienced as a 10-year old embedded itself into the cells of my body. I have now had the memories removed from my cells. They are gone. Those unhealthy memories that have embedded themselves into the cells of my body from the time my father wrapped his arm around my throat and choked the air from my body. They are gone! I want health for my life.

I try to eat right, why? So I can attain health. Some things go beyond what I put into my mouth. I strive for a good life. I must give myself a solid foundation for a chance at overall health. In order to build a sturdy house, we lay down concrete so it will be steady, firm, and handle a great house. A strong foundation must be set. This is what I am doing for myself. I have to rebuild my foundation.

In Numbers 14:18 we read, "The LORD is slow to anger, abounding in love and forgiving sin and rebellion. Yet he does not leave the guilty unpunished; he punishes the children for the sin of the parents to the third and fourth generation."." Make no mistake, God loves us. He does wish for us to have health and well-being. We have to do our parts. I have had to search for my optimal health.

I must admit I am finding less of the old memories as my new habits are becoming embedded into my thinking. I have learned what is good for me and what is not. After a toxic relationship, coming to Dallas, I immediately started the healing process for getting out of these types of relationships. I went to al-anon. I learned how to say "no" but be able to do it with love in my heart. Always before, it was a fight I put up in order to say "no". I needed conflict in order to say "no". There had to be an extreme conflict, yet I want to have peace in my heart? This doesn't make sense.

Love is about bringing out the best in another and seeing them become their best. I have love for my Lady Friend and I know she has love for her Adventure Partner as she calls me.

HEALING BEGINS WITH GIVING:

I started giving back. It ties into my childhood. I hit a wall when my relationship with my father hit its wall. He couldn't lead me anymore to reach goals. I needed guidance and direction to fulfill my dreams. I didn't get that when I was in my teenage years, though I knew there were others in this world rowing the same boat as me. They had dreams and needed someone to show them the trail to finding their dreams and goals. I knew there were people –

Robert Santi, Donna Spicer, Uncle Tommy and Aunt Dodie, Uncle Jimmy and Aunt Penny, and an Argo family – who helped me when they didn't have to. They provided homes for me when I didn't have one as a teenager because dad kicked me out of the house. As he told me, "Don't come back." And I didn't many times.

Those people put their neck out on the line for me. I knew I couldn't repay them specifically but I could pay it forward. I could help someone else. I could help guide a lost sheep to find their way. It made me a better man serving other people. Thank you to anyone and everyone who helped me and let me help them. I learned how to become of service to others.

There was an acronym I saw once and it has stuck with me

T.E.A.M.

Together
Everyone
Achieves
More

Journey of the Son

To all of us who have taken the abuse – if you're doing it to someone else, meaning you are doing the same thing that was done to you – why are doing it to the ones who love you and the ones you love? Build them up, don't beat them down. Build a foundation so they too can go on and find the fulfillment life has for them.

We are supposed to know better as adults. Equip yourself to fight against your hurts and how life has hurt you; we all have the anger on the inside. Stop the violence to the innocent. A child has a precious soul and parents are supposed to be protectors of the innocence in their soul.

You have the courage to stand strong – to stand up against whoever told you that you're not worth it. You have the courage – it's there even if you haven't found it yet. If I can do it, so can you. I always believed in actions, not words. That is why I chose mentors who walk their talk not just talk their talk.

A New Beginning

Life will have its ups and downs. Even when things seem to have completely turned around, disappointment will reappear at some point, sadly often much sooner than you are ready.

After I had consciously began giving back and began using my coaching method with the motto of T.E.A.M my greatest disappointment was yet to come. In 2000 I fell short of making the Olympic trials. I was devastated! My last chance before I aged out and I just blew it. I let distractions get in my way of a life-long goal. Discouragement followed with questions like: Why do I have all these disappointments? Where is my fulfillment? Why am I continually putting roadblocks in my way?

This played right into my self-esteem as I grew up feeling unworthy. This is what abusers are able to pass on to their offspring. I can have a difficult time believing I am worthy of any type of success.

To me, the failure of not making the 2000 Olympic Trials in the 400m Hurdles is really a result of my actions leading into that misfire.

It has taken me years to let go and realize that not reaching that life goal does not make me a failure. I heard it said that failure is an event, not a person and that is so true. Every person fails in life at some point. No one is exempt. You will blow it and it will be your own fault. Accept it and move on.

This realization actually brings comfort to me knowing we are not out there by ourselves – that "there is someone else out there just like me. Maybe I am not so screwed up".

The Indian proverb that sticks with me: a wise grandfather and his grandson. The grandson says to his wise grandfather, "Grandpa, Grandpa there are these two wolves fighting in my head. One wolf is a good wolf and the other wolf is a bad wolf. Grandpa, which one wins?"

The wise grandfather looks at his grandson and replies, "The one you feed the most."

As we go about our day, what wolf are we feeding the most?

James 3 addresses the power of the tongue and the need to control such a small body part:

"We all stumble in many ways. Anyone who is never at fault in what they say is perfect, able to keep their whole body in check. When we put bits into the mouths of horses to make them obey us, we can turn the whole animal. ⁴ Or take ships as an example. Although they are so large and are driven by strong winds, they are

steered by a very small rudder wherever the pilot wants to go. ⁵ Likewise, the tongue is a small part of the body, but it makes great boasts. Consider what a great forest is set on fire by a small spark. ⁶ The tongue also is a fire, a world of evil among the parts of the body. It corrupts the whole body, sets the whole course of one's life on fire, and is itself set on fire by hell..." James 3:2-6 NIV.

There is power in the tongue. What one says will determine the course of one's life. As a coach, I adopted the policy that "I don't believe a word you say. I believe everything your actions say." I have had athletes tell me until they are blue in the face how great they are going to become, yet I have seen them do many contradictory actions that deterred them from their success on the field. We are all guilty.

There are some of us for whom the truth is as foreign as vegetables are to the American diet. And there are others who supply the right foods to their diet and they are unashamed to wear their bathing suit. It's an analogy.

The media looks to set fires among us, the people. And what do we do? We keep watching the news outlets while looking for the wars and the problems. I simply turned off the news and stopped watching it. It does not lift me up as a person and I have enough of the bad wolf in me. I really do not need to feed him any more than what my eyes and ears already pick up.

In the reticular activation system, your brain picks up everything around. The brain then deciphers what we need to recognize. If we picked up everything that is actually going on around us we would go into sensory overload. What we feed the bad and good wolves determines how our reticular activation system will be energized. We're picking it all up, but there is only so much we can acknowledge.

Out of darkness light must come. We will demand it. There is only so much we will tolerate as a whole. Then we will crave the light. We will say that it is time for something different. We will get sick of dealing with all the difficulties we are voluntarily putting on ourselves – and that is what we are doing when we are living in turmoil. The light will have its voice. How did the Niagara Falls start? It had to have started with one drop of water and now more than 168,000 cubic meters (6 million cubic feet) of water that go over the crestline of the falls every minute during peak daytime tourist hours. How was Rome built? Brick by brick. It is a process.

This is true with a society and with us as individuals. Michael Jackson stated it best with his song, "Man in the Mirror." This is where it starts for all of us. We look at the man in the mirror and start seeking the best for the person we see in the mirror's reflection.

THE EMPIRE STRIKES BACK

What happens when things go wrong? And I do mean when things go wrong, not if they go wrong! When that happens you have a choice—every choice you make affects your future from that moment on. Good or bad, it directs the next step of your journey.

Well, once again, things did not go as planned for me. I wanted certain things and when they didn't come to pass, I nonetheless stayed faithful. I was healing and I was making better choices so I was able to be faithful in the midst of disappointment. I believed in the promises of God. Obviously, trust has been quite an issue for me in my life. I stayed true to what the Bible was telling me. Matthew 5:13 states, "But if salt loses its saltiness, how can it

Journey of the Son

be made salty again?" This was a motivator for me as a man in my 20s and early 30s to keep true to the course. Let me describe how that verse speaks to me. I interpreted those words to say: If I mess up, then I may lose my innocence; then, what good am I to God? I wanted to keep my purity for God. I wanted to keep my purity for my soul. I was afraid of not knowing what it is like to have God's blessing on my life. I was afraid to challenge this principle. I stayed true to the Word as best as I could. I trusted God with my life.

And then...things went wrong. Life got tougher. The gray line started to appear; it wasn't so black and white any more. I started living in the gray area.

I didn't make the Olympic trials as I had wanted to so badly. I didn't make a ton of money, but I had stature. I had respect within the community and from those whom I trained. Daggers started coming at me from opponents. False accusations and rumors. I let them get to me a bit. I wasn't a good business man and trained many people for free. Why? Because they asked for help and I knew they couldn't afford it. I didn't charge this one running back a single dollar. He was in college. I didn't think college kids had much money and what little they had, they needed it to eat. Well, that running back went on to be an NFL first round draft pick. What I taught him definitely helped him in setting NCAA records. I am not about to tell you I "made" this guy. God gave this individual great talent, strength, and explosion – the best I have ever seen. I showed him how to get the most out of those attributes when it came to running and also how to disguise his speed. Therefore, he could bait an angle from a linebacker or defensive end. Once the defensive player committed to an angle, the running back could change his gears and slip right by them and down the sideline. Then he would go for many, many yards. I ended up living in a garage without a car. He ended up living in mansions with many exotic cars.

Then there was my dad whom I didn't rely on for anything. Maybe I didn't want any certain tangible things from him particularly as time went on. I just wanted him to be my father. I wanted to have someone I could trust and go to for advice when things went into unknown territory. It would have been nice, but I didn't have a father I could turn to. I couldn't trust him with my heart because he would use this against me. What I had was the ability to look at his life and know the decisions he made and tell myself to do the opposite. I didn't respect the decisions he had made. I didn't want to follow in his footsteps. This relationship allowed me to be aware I am at the mercy of the Lord. Yes, God provided for me. I have been homeless before. But I never went without. I have always been provided with good friends and some very loving family members in my life. My grandmother and my Aunt Dodie are angels to me. My grandmother in some ways was my guardian angel. My Aunt Dodie's love brought me back from the abyss of my life.

In my abyss, I found my anger toward God. My life didn't go as expected. I wanted to take God on personally. I wanted to stare him in the face and let him know that I trusted in him and it didn't go as my heart desired. I just about wanted to hit God. I did with my words. All my anger went inwardly and turned into my darkest days. I even wanted to kill myself, yet again. At one time or two, I prayed for death. I can remember thinking, "If my best days are behind me, let me die." I don't want to be a great warrior who fought one battle and then went to "pasture." I wanted more triumphs in life. I had more battles to win. I didn't feel that way anymore as I laid in that dark garage – in that bed for 12 hours at a time. I really wanted to die. I couldn't kill myself because my family would not be able to tolerate it. In a way, my dad's suicide attempt saved my life. If I had not seen firsthand what a suicide attempt does to a family, I might have done it to myself.

So what did I do? I went to war with God for a time. If he is the Maker, then he is responsible for all of this that goes on here on earth. He allowed evil to happen. He is the Creator of all, so I reasoned that he therefore is responsible. When something goes wrong on a sports team, who is responsible? The Head Coach. It is their responsibility to right the ship and if they can't, they get to meet with Donald Trump for the "You're Fired!" meeting. So, I decided that I was firing God in my life. "Hey, God, step into my office. I didn't make the Olympic Trials. My dad shot himself. I don't have dollar to my name. YOU'RE FIRED!"

I can remember when I got my foot on the ground from my darkest day. The one where it felt like a gorilla was sitting on my chest. That's when I found out that we might not see everything such as depression or stress, but it is very real. We only see the side effects of what depression is. It weighs more than a gorilla. It fights harder than a gorilla. Both can kill you. Depression almost killed me. Once my foot hit the ground, I started my comeback. My comeback was something I had to do on my own. I had to do it my way. It has taken some time for me to develop trust in God once more, but I do have it again. It is a relationship. If we are not allowed to have a say, then it is not a relationship, but a dictatorship. We, especially Americans, love our freedom. We want to have the ability to have a choice. This is evident as you look throughout our country. Whether we are right or wrong, we want the ability of choice. I exercised this choice as a Christian. I exercised a choice and by the grace of God I was able to find out he loved me all the while. I may have thought I wasn't worthy of love but his love never ceased to exist. This means a lot to me. Even in my stubbornness, in my rebellion, his love is still there. He never gave up on me. My earthly father did.

Believe What You Think

I accepted something during that time: God made me. He didn't make me to be somebody else. He uniquely made me. I have a walk to make in my life. Sometimes I will make it easy, and other times I will make it hard on myself. Either way, God still loves me through it all.

Grace is a concept that I had no idea about until I had a child out of wedlock. I thought I would be stoned or that God would walk out on me, but neither happened. I prayed for love, to know love. By my perceived failures I started to find out about love at greater depths, depths I did not give myself permission to think existed. I only found out about these depths of love through my failures. Thankfully, I do know love through successes, but it is through failures that I have a greater depth about love. I think it lies somewhere in the fact that conventional religion teaches us that if we mess up, we are going to experience God's wrath – lightning bolts from the sky will virtually strike us down! Not true.

Take a deep breath and stop thinking for a few moments. Just meditate on this simple truth: God loves us. He doesn't love me any more in my mistakes than in my achievements. I think we tend to feel more worthy of love in our triumphs. We tend to tell ourselves we are not worthy of love in our mistakes. Both are false. His love is available for us 24/7/365.

Jesus came to heal a hurting world. Jesus said "It is not the healthy who need a doctor, but the sick. I have not come to call the righteous, but sinners to repentance." (Luke 5:31-32) A prostitute came begging at his feet, cleaned his feet with her hair. She wanted healing. She wanted forgiveness. She was desperate for it. He forgave her and showed much compassion and love for her. This woman is one of those women you wouldn't want to be seen with in public. People will whisper about you even talking to a woman such as this. People will question your reputation if you even speak with such an individual. Why? Because in many of our minds even these people are beneath Jesus' healing. But no, Jesus didn't think that way. He had greater compassion than average men. He didn't condemn the woman and he didn't condemn me even though I wanted to hit him, I was so angry.

I do know in my heart, when I am following the path that is best for me and my growth; I have peace and trust I both am enough and I have enough.

Regarding the tongue: we have the good

wolf and the bad wolf. As I have said, it comes down to these simple words: As a man thinketh so he becomes. The other side to this statement is to Believe what you think. If you do so, you will believe what you think and you will become what you think. One will crave the reality his/her thoughts are driving them toward.

This sounds like an obvious statement but I am challenging you to ask yourself if you really believe what you think you think.

Chapter 9

Walls Come Tumbling Down

Therapy – have you ever been? Needless to say, I have. Yes, I have been to plenty of therapy. I started going about the age of 15. I am one of those who doesn't mind speaking with someone. I sort of have this curiosity about life. I want to know what others are thinking. As a child, I would always ask my father, "Why?" I would then ask "why" to his answer. It definitely kept the car ride full of conversation. If Dad got sick of answering "why," he would just say "because I said so." That was his way of saying, "I'm tired of thinking right now." I just had this curiosity as to why things happened. I've always been a people watcher and I love observing life.

Curiosity is also a very helpful tool in creating a character for acting. Why do I brush my teeth with my left hand, then switch to my right and add toothpaste at that time? Why is that? There is always a reason. The reason why I brush my teeth with my left hand is because it is my off hand. I read an article stating that brushing your teeth with your opposite hand will help stimulate the other side of your brain and help coordination. I also read that brushing your teeth first without toothpaste will help stimulate the removal of plaque on the teeth. See, there is always a "why" to why we do things.

My stepmother thought I should see a therapist. When I got to see a therapist at the age of 15, it was a relief, I thought. I could no longer speak with anyone at home. At least here was an adult I could speak with and be honest. I could have open dialogue and not be judged or punished. A wiser man could help me find my answers. By the way, this was a psychologist; I do not believe in taking the pills so I can numb myself to deal with life. Human nature is flawed and we live in an imperfect world. I could not trust or speak with my father. This is why I looked forward to speaking with another adult.

I recently experienced a therapy session while writing this memoir. I had not seen a therapist in a long, long time. I thought I was going to receive prayer, healing prayer over any disconnect in my life, between me and the Maker. It felt like a therapy session. This woman was able to take me down a road that led Father God to be my therapist. I shut my eyes and could feel the words coming to my heart. She would pray over what was being told to me, what the "Voice" was telling me.

Eventually, I was led to seeing a little boy who locked himself into a room. There was a wooden chair, dust on the floor, a wooden table, and a window. The little boy was curled in a ball with his back up against the door. He was scared, very scared. He didn't want to let anyone in. He was protecting himself by locking the door and putting his weight against it. His head was tucked into his chest, clutching his knees, squeezing them into his body. It was me. I envision myself for a moment as a child: my bowl cut hairdo, olive skin, and the much tinier nose that I had back then. (I have broken this thing one too many times).

I have lived in this room for all of my life. I have gotten comfortable accepting my surroundings in this room. It is safe. I have made it safe for myself. All of the fear that has held me prisoner is in that room.

Do you know how hard it is to change

something you have known all your life? This woman prayed: "Father God, what is it you want Marcus to see?" I could see him come in and take my hand. He wanted to take me out of this room. Out into the light. He wanted to take me for a walk in the rest of the world while I was resting in his security, in his love. I did, I was – and then I felt the darkness surround me. It didn't want to let go. It has held me prisoner in that room for so long. It doesn't want to let go of me or I don't want to let go of it. I became disconnected from my vision. I couldn't feel the Light. Then, in the midst of my darkness, a tunnel of light appeared. I had to crawl through this tunnel of light to get to a world full of light. I got right to the edge and I didn't want to come out. I just wanted to stay right there, a few feet from being surrounded by the light. I was good with knowing that there is light. I ask myself, am I still scared? Am I too scared to trust the one who made me? How scared am I?

I felt like this cat that I was around; he would sit in your lap and love on you. Then, he would just jump off and go hide behind the couch. There were times and I would try to get him to come out. "It's okay, you can come on out." He would just look, something would spook him, and of course, there were times when he just wanted to be left alone. He'd hiss at me then. I felt like the cat. But someone had harmed the cat. The owner's son, a complete and utter hellion. He had no regard for others and the hell he inflicted on them. Why does God make these people? Well they are here in this world and we have to deal with them. Supposedly with love. WHY? There I go again with my "whys."

GENERATIONAL CURSES & TRACK RECORDS

In my life I have fought and fought, mostly in my mind and in my soul. I never want to see another man suffer by the result of my hand. My anger can take me to emotional places where I would love to see a man bleed as the result of my hand but I do not act on it. "Marcus" I remember reading is a derivative of "Mars" and what is "Mars" in the Roman mythology? He is the god of war. I have found many wars with others and within myself throughout the course of my life. I thought it was appropriate and poetic that my name is after the god of war. I would like to think it was more from the likes of Marcus Aurelius which according to the movie Gladiator only knew peace four years out of his 20 years of being Caesar.

Maybe I was the perfect candidate for my dad as a son? Maybe I was the perfect candidate for my family? Something needed to be put to an end. The violence and the verbal abuse the men brought to the family, at least my branch of the family tree. I do not ever remember my grandfather saying anything hurtful to me. I have just heard so many stories of the countless fighting between him and my father.

The shit that followed my dad, I saw and felt. In turn he passed, by way of actions, this negative behavior on to me (generational curse). He tried to blow his brains out. I sure wanted to blow my own brains out a number of times. He abused his wives. I never took one. I will say that my grandfather did not abuse my grandmother. I think he would rot in hell if he ever did as she was an angel. I don't know where my dad got all of his rage from. He could take it to a level 12 out of a possible 10. That was his personality – he did everything big.

In the Bible, there are certain numbers that seem to be associated with being holy or "magical": 3, 7, and 40. It has taken me somewhere around 40 years to figure some things out in my life. I have not mastered life, but who has? I like where I am. Every now and again I create wars to keep myself from getting bored. For example, on my birthdays I find a "physical test" to accomplish. Usually, it consists of lifting some massive weight (dead lifting 400lbs) or sprinting a 400. There are those numbers again 4-0.

When it comes to battle, I really think it gets down to how far one is willing to go in order to win. How much pain can one tolerate and… ignore. When you think you cannot take another step, yet you do. That is the one who is usually going to win. Make pain your friend, make it nonexistent. That is what I did on the track. My "want to" outweighed my pain.

The other side of the coin is to be smart with efforts. Moderate pain really isn't there. It's only there if you declare it to be there. I think for so many years that I thought I needed the pain in various forms. I believe I got this from religion: Jesus Christ suffered and if we are followers of Him we must suffer as well. I don't believe this anymore. Jesus took on a burden and I certainly am not Jesus Christ. I don't need to be Jesus Christ if I am to believe in him. Just because he suffered doesn't mean I have to go looking for it. I am Marcus Santi uniquely made. I have my plot in life and I believe "as man thinks so he becomes." If I seek pain, then I will find it. If I seek love I will find it. I have had great pains in my life. To some degree, I sought the pain as I thought I deserved it. I let that abuse from my father go on with me even after the fact. I wanted to be angry at him. It was my edge for so many years. "Now these three remain: faith, hope, and love. The greatest is love." It didn't mention anger or hate in this Bible verse. The longer I held onto my hate and anger the more war I found and the more unrest I found.

Prozac is so prevalent in society. It's part of our thought life. Our mind works the same way our body does. If we eat crappy food, then we should not expect to get the ripped six pack abs. If we watch and read crap do not expect our thought life to foster a garden of love, peace, and harmony. As a man thinks, so he becomes.

My thought life for so many years consisted of hatred and anger toward my father; my inner life was filled with pain and turmoil. Forgiveness led to more love and peace within my heart. I can run a 400m sprint today and not hurt. I can sprint with peace in my heart. Translation: I can move about with peace and love in my heart. I don't need pain to motivate me.

Chapter 10

The Gold Medal

Here is the most imporant gold medal of all of my life: MY BROTHER.

When I look back upon this experience, I would say that it is moments like the one this photo was able to capture which are more gratifying than a gold medal. The love is what makes it more valuable than a gold medal experience.

When I was 4, 5, and 6 years old, I would pray with my mother. My prayer was to have a younger brother. I was 5 and I didn't think about the logistics of what it took to make a baby. Mom was single at that time, and since then I have learned quite well that you do not have to be married to make a baby. I wanted a younger brother. I don't remember if I stopped praying for this as I got older into my early teen years.

I do remember standing right next to Mom when she got off of the phone with her doctor and she was in utter shock. As she was hanging up the phone and she said, "I'm pregnant," I can remember my first words out of my mouth: "How did that happen?" Mom's next comment was, "Didn't your father have this conversation with you?"

In the midst of choas, we all are given a gift. My life was in a place where I was contemplating suicide. My relationship with my mother was awful. My relationship with my father was abusive. I wanted out of this life. My mother's life was no better. As she was pregnant with Patrick, supressed memories of being abused and molested came rushing back to her. Her second marriage was going down the tubes, heading for divorce.

Again, in the midst of all this chaos, we all were given a gift. My stepfather was given his only son. My mother was given an opportunity to mother a child in better circumstances than what she was given with me. I was given the brother I always prayed for. I was given a

Journey of the Son

reason to love and a reason to live.

God heard my prayer and just at the right time in our lives, he answered my prayer. He provided us with the greatest gift we could have been given. I have always considered my brother the greatest gift God has ever blessed me with. I love my brother. I helped raise him. His presence gave me a reason to stay alive.

When mom had Patrick, I went up to the hospital the next day. I was anxious to see what he looked like, hesitant at the same time as well. I was 15, I got to miss school and watch the NCAA basketball tournament – that excited me a ton. The nurses brought him in to see us. It was just mom and me in the room. Mom asked if I would like to hold him. I was reluctant. I didn't know what to do, so I just observed. He looked like an alien bird. I just sat with Mom and eventually she made me hold him. I did, and all fears subsided. I looked into his eyes and then just looked at him. I will never forget the moment that changed my life forever. I reached out for his tiny little hand with my finger and he grabbed my finger. Everything changed from that moment on. The light of the room became brighter. It was as if cobwebs, haze, were lifted from my eyes and I could see again.

Marcus Santi

After this moment, I would get out of my bed for about two years only because I wanted to be a great big brother. My prayers began to go like: "Dear God, let me be the best brother I can be for Patrick." I remember that was one of my biggest goals in life. It was the only reason why I got out of bed in the morning many days. I knew I had to if I wanted to be a great brother to Patrick. I was depressed, but being with him brought me joy. I was living in my truth when I was around him. I didn't care about what people thought of me when I was with him. It was just us; I knew we were going to have a bunch of fun together.

Looking back, my little brother knew I would let him be mischievous. Heck, I was the master at it. I taught it to him. We would run errands with mom and when she would go into the store, I would let Patrick do whatever he wanted to in the car. I would put him in the driver's seat when Mom would run into the store. I would teach him what the dashboard did, the windshield wipers, blinkers, etc. This became one of our things. We would act as bored as could be when Mom was parking the car. She would say, "I'll be right back; y'all wait in here." Patrick had the part down. He would look out the window as if he barely heard her.

Journey of the Son

As soon as Mom was out of the door, Patrick came to life, panting, getting himself unbuckled from his car seat, and bull rushing the front seat. He would stand up in the seat, grab hold of the steering wheel, turn on the lights, blinkers, windshield wipers, and jump up and down in the driver's seat. Then this would crack me up: he would take his head and spear the middle of the steering wheel and blast the horn of the car. He would press his head so hard into the horn and hold it there for long periods of time. It was hilarious.

I was the look out. I'd let him know when I would see Mom coming out of the store. As soon as she was spotted, he would quickly jump back into his car seat and buckle himself in. He could do all of this before he ever said his first word. Mom would get in the car and we were back to the "bored as all get out" look. She would turn the ignition and everything would come on in the car. We would burst out laughing. And of course the high fives were exchanged as well.

I wanted him and he wanted me. I learned, amazingly, as he was getting older not to push my wants and desires for myself onto him. I did feel like I was a big part of raising this young man. I didn't want my success as an athlete and trainer in my community to overshadow him or have him feel like he needed to live up to some image I had for him. We successfully kept those parts of our lives separated.

Whenever we did anything, we did it as a team. We played basketball in the driveway as a team against the air. We learned our lesson about competing against one another. You want to know how we learned this lesson?

There was such an age gap that there wasn't much for us to compete against one another in. Video games were our outlet. We played John Madden football and he beat me one particular game. I would always let him stay close to me and it would be a last-second victory. Not this time. He kicked my butt. He was doing his little dance and rubbing it in my face. Well, he woke up the sleeping bear.

I took it seriously and I goaded him into another game. Yeah, the score was 55 to just about nothing. I was stuffing him left and right. It was "go time" baby. Aren't I *so* mature? I started doing my dance and mimicking what he did to me. We never finished the game, I made him cry. I'm sorry I couldn't help it. I do have such a competitor within me. I felt like, "if you can't take it, don't dish it out." I was making a point. He was rubbing my face in it; I, in turn, taught him what it felt like.

We never competed like that against one another again. That was fine by me. I didn't want to compete with him. I wanted a teammate.

I learned how important a foundation is. I did my part in helping my brother have a great foundation.

I remember feeling like my brother didn't need me so much when he hit his teen years. Now, he is an adult in his 20s. I have to remind myself that we still need each other. We are many miles apart and rarely get to see one another. No matter what the age, we are brothers.

On the same street, going into the same finish line, I was blessed with the opportunity to do what my dad did with me: I was able to run with my younger brother through the finish line of a 5K race. He was about the same age I was in that photo with my father as I was sprinting into the line. When I look back upon this experience, I would say that it is moments like the one this photo was able to capture which are more gratifying than a gold medal. The love is what makes it more valuable than a gold medal experience.

All I knew was that *this is my little brother*. Back when he was 3 and 4, he didn't like it when I would call him my little brother. I was explaining to him how he was my little brother. He actually thought I was calling *him* little. He didn't like being called little, and would tell me that I was his little brother. He would climb up the shelves of the cubboard and get eye to eye with me and tell me "See! Now you're my YITTLE BROTHER." He couldn't say his "L's" at that point in time. I got a real kick out of it. He was born an old soul outside of a few hang ups as a child which he outgrew pretty quickly .

Patrick's existence brought pure love to my life. He loved me, and I loved him purely. There was no harm that tainted our love for one another. I had never experienced this before. From this relationship, I was given the gift of knowing what real love is. This is a brotherly love, but nonetheless it is a pure love. Most all my loves in my life outside of my brother, grandmother, and Aunt Dodie have all been conditional.

"Now these three remain: faith, hope, and love" (I Corinthians 13:13). My brother allowed for this verse to play out in my life. I had **hope** that I would have a brother, I had **faith** in my younger years that God would bless me with my prayer of a younger brother, and I was shown **love** by the relationship with my younger brother – not a little brother, really, but a younger brother. Yes, I am taller than he is, so technically, Patrick you are my little brother – but it's no big deal, you have more hair than I do!

I have been able to find completeness in my life with love. I have found it with my mother, and I even found it with my father. Some paths are much easier to travel than others. Some of us are difficult to love, and we make it difficult to love. It is there, but we must have the courage, the patience, and the persistance to seek it out. I have yet to find a wife, and I am not sure if marriage is something for me. At least for now, it is not. I am happy regardless. Why? The three people I have mentioned have loved me freely and I have been given the opportunity to love them freely. They want nothing in return from me. They just love me and in turn it is easy to love them and to trust them with my love.

Chapter 11

GUARDIAN ANGEL:

With all that I've been through—all the abuse, rejection and betrayal—one of the ways God let me know he was real is by sending me my guardian angel in the flesh. She was my Grandmother Josephine--affectionately known as Josephine The Flying Machine Annaratone Santi. She loved me no matter what I did and she saved my life. She took me in when I had no home to go to. This allowed me to finish high school. She provided a safety net which allowed me to pursue my dreams wholeheartedly and help others pursue their dreams in athletics. There is always someone behind the scenes who is the backbone who allows another to find the champion within themselves. Grandma was my backbone. I was 19 and I had no home. My father had left town and I was on my own. I had not completed high school then due to my wilderness extrvaganza. I had to go an extra semester of high school. I did the 5-year plan. I will never forget I went to Grandma's to get a good meal and I was leaving not knowing where I was going. She told me "Honey, you live here now." Her plan was to give me a good home and I was going to finish high school and go on to college. That was her plan. I liked the plan as well.

I will admit the only thing I loved about college; beside football games, friends, and women was the fact that I could pursue my goal of running track at a university. I didn't go for a formal education, I went to run track. I did school because I had to in order to be eligible so I could run in track meets.

My Guardian Angel gave me a home, and lots of food, particularly pasta as only Grandma could prepare it and say it. Her belly bounced like a basketball as she would say to me "Marc, I made you some PASTA! It's the BEST! The BEST I ever made!" She was so proud of her pasta. I will say I stopped eating pasta after she passed away. Why? Because I never tasted any pasta, except for when I went to Italy, that could rival my grandmother's.

She kept me healthy with her love and her pasta. She kept the whole world around me

Journey of the Son

healthy with her pasta. Anyone of my friends who knew me ate my grandmother's pasta. My best friend Kevin Argo, who does not like pasta, liked my grandmother's pasta. It was her way of showing her love and she carried a good amount of pride in how good her pasta was.

Everyone knew my grandma; if they knew me, then they knew her. I think my whole family is like that. All my friends know my Aunt Dodie and Aunt Rita and if you hang out long enough they will stick into your memory for a lifetime. My father was the same way. My dad came and spoke at a business class of mine and from that some of my other friends started asking my dad to come to speak to some of their other classes as well. My family is fun. I know there was tragedy in this story as I started writing this book. To me the tragedy is that we didn't allow the good times to be all the time with my dad and me. My grandmother had the purest heart I have come across. She just loved everyone. People remember her because she loved you. She was harmless. She was a breath of fresh air.

When someone would leave, it didn't matter who it was, she would send them out the door with cookies and she would say to them, "Love you sweetie. Thank you." I asked her "Grandma, how can you love this person when you don't know them?" Her reply "I don't know, I just do." At 20 something I didn't really understand how that was. Today at 40-something, I understand better: her heart was pure and she really meant what she said. She didn't know any other way to be. This is who she was and she was true to her heart. She had a great heart and she lived from it. This is why she is my Guardian Angel. She put life in me with her love and her actions. She saved me and built me over.

I shake my head because I don't how dad got so tainted in his heart? Did he take his mother for granted? I know I did as I did not fully appreciate everything about her sweetness at the time. I had things I wanted to do. I took it to a point and before I went too far, her sweetness that she passed onward to me kicked in. Dad, I don't know how much sweetness he had.

While living with my grandmother, I flourished and thrived. I achieved some really good things – things that defied today's standards when it came to coaching and leading individuals. I didn't follow the Pied Piper that most people flow with, perhaps three quarters of this world. I chose to follow the best. I wanted to learn from the best. Grandma was the best when it came to loving others. Once again I refer to I Corinthians 13:13: "Now these three remain: faith, hope, and love. The greatest of which is love." With love, and through love, we can do anything.

I left college after I ran my last track meet. I didn't bother to finish; I hated school. Through destiny, I started to train people on how to be faster. It grew. I have been hired so many times at jobs in which one is to be a college graduate. The job pertained to speed development and/or training the human body and mind. I have been asked to teach other trainers, who have their degrees and possibly master's degrees from college – to do what I do with my athletes. My athletes went above and beyond what the 80% of this world thought they could or should be capable of attaining.

My Guardian Angel's love allowed me to act upon what was already inside of me. I knew it was in me and that I just needed the support so I could channel this to the world.

The world with my father left me engulfed in fear. I couldn't reach this place within me because I was exerting energy and thoughts dealing with my own insecurities with my home life which my father left me with. My Grandmother within the span of a few short years reversed all of this negative training I received at my father's household and allowed me to go about life with the mighty warrior within me. I was loved enough so I could go about my day with the heart of love and passion I was given. No more supression to keep this side of me burried. Grandma allowed me to go about life with my heart.

This is what happens when one grows up in a home of love and nurturing. The best within them steps out the door and goes out into the world. This makes the world a better place when we are out there taking steps to the greater good of mankind. Josephine Anaratone Santi is a real Angel. She is one whom God smiles upon with many great moments. She may not have built any concrete building and slapped her name on it, rather, she built people. Her love gave me a home to come home to. It was full and complete.

The Eulogy

My dad did pass away and he did so peacefully. He had what one might consider a good death. This is a man who took a bullet to the head and fought for his life after an attempt to take it. During his recovery, he had multiple mini strokes while in intensive care. He caught MRSA (a super bad staph infection) and on top of that, he had pneumonia. Supposedly, MRSA is enough to kill and so is pneumonia on its own. He had both at the same time along with a fresh bullet wound to the head. He survived this not once, but twice.

He was bull-headed in so many ways. This helped keep him alive. For seven years, he lay in a bed not being able to really move. There were intermittent moments of speech. I realized once my father made it out of the woods, after the first 6 weeks of recovery, God had something left for my father to learn here in this world. Albert could slash you to pieces with his tongue. He would always strike first, even when there was no reason to strike. It was his protection mode. He had a hard time accepting another person's love. His tongue got so bad, after two failed marriages and three kids who did not want anything to do with him; I don't think he could allow himself to be loved.

I know a lot of his thoughts dwelled on why his father hit him and on why his father was so abusive toward him. Dad let a lot of those thoughts dictate his life. It made him insecure. You combine that with selfish desires and I guess you get a suicide attempt. He was lonely. He was ALONE by his own doing.

My dad needed peace in his life. He was too good at causing conflict in and around him. Ironically, his tongue was taken from him. Albert's ability to move, his physical abilities, were taken from him. He had no choice but to rely on those around him.

The day I received a phone call telling me that my dad passed, I was doing a morning meditation. In my meditation, I had found some angry thoughts toward my father, feelings about him hitting me and how those actions stripped me of my courage as a child and how they have affected me today. I really thought I had long

Journey of the Son

forgiven my father and I know I have. Every now and again those negative memories come back to me. In my meditation I spoke with my father. I saw him in my mind lying there in his hospital bed. I talked to his heart. I told him, "Dad, yes, I get angry from time to time because you hit me. I don't know why you did it. I want you to know dad, I love you. I do, I love you dad. I forgive you for hitting me. It's alright. We are fine, Dad. I just want you to know that. I'm sorry for getting angry at you. Bye, dad. I love you."

About an hour later, I was sitting in the kitchen and a wall of light swept right by me and went out the door. I visually saw it move right out the door. The door to the backyard opened as the light exited the door. My naked eyes saw no physical person, but the door flew open.

That afternoon, my aunt called me and told me that Albert passed away. It was a peaceful death. After so many traumas he had experienced in his life, he went in such a peaceful manner. It was very simple: his heart rate started to accelerate and he simply passed on. He let go of his body. He learned what he needed to learn. He accepted love and I believe he made peace with his father as well. He made peace with his existence. It was the one lesson he needed to learn all of his life. He learned it and he then could move on.

He left this world knowing love. Isn't this the greatest thing we could have as we leave this world?

I was asked to deliver his eulogy. I was not mad at my father, and I have long forgiven him. I wanted to leave my father in his glory through being given this responsibility. I needed to find his glory. What was I overlooking? What did I not appreciate about our relationship while he was alive?

I listened. I knew the people around him would tell me to reveal how Albert affected their lives. I heard a whole lot of what an excellent story teller he was, what a great joke teller he was, and how he loved racing cars, playing tennis, and University of Memphis Tiger football games and basketball games. I heard all of what I knew. I wanted to find something I didn't know about my dad. I found it.

I asked God before I went to bed, "Show me what makes my dad beautiful. Allow me to see and find my dad's beauty." I have this belief

Journey of the Son

that we have love in our hearts. When we find our love, think with our love, we find our beauty. We ask nothing in return. We serve our fellow man and we wish for this world to be a better place. I wanted to find my dad's heart.

God answered my prayer. He showed me three stories that define my father's heart.

I was six years old at the time, and my father believed in staying fit and eating right. He passed that on to me. He would always take me jogging around the campus of Rhodes College. It was a little over three miles. It was a long, long way for 6-year-old legs to keep up with my father's 5'9" adult legs.

There was this one run, and I was hurting. I was having difficulty breathing due to a side stitch. I was complaining. "Dad, dad, I can't breathe. It hurts so badly. Dad, let's stop." He did stop. He turned around and looked me square in my eyeballs and he said something to me that I will never ever forget. "Son, don't you ever give up. I don't care how bad it hurts, no matter how bad the pain gets, DON'T YOU EVER GIVE UP." When he said this to me, I knew he meant it with every fiber of his being. From that moment forward I believed with all of my being. Why? Because my Superman said so; I knew he was telling me the truth.

That moment changed my life for the better. This was 1978 – long before Jim Valvano's great ESPY speech. I received my own Jimmy V speech before there was a Jimmy V speech. That statement has driven me up to many mountain tops. I learned to never put my head on my pillow at night living in regret because I wasn't my best. I had to be my best. My best might be good enough to win the race, win the league championship, or win at work. I learned each day to try to make myself better than what I was the day before. Albert passed what was true in his heart on to me, which made this possible for me to understand the concept: my mental body will dictate my physical body; my physical body will not dictate my mental body.

Albert has a sister named Rita. She is a very gifted teacher who works with the hearing impaired. Every year she directs a play. These are truly great productions. Due to a family trait, she is meticulous in coordinating the performance. I am sure she stays awake at night thinking over every segment of the play and how to bring out the best in her actors. As she sleeps, I am sure she dreams about it as well.

Journey of the Son

This is exhausting — these types of efforts. She pours her all into her work. At the end of every year, when the play was over, she would say to Albert, "That's it. That is my last production. I can't do it anymore." Albert attended her productions every year. He loved to watch them. He would tell Rita "You keep going. You can do it." He knew Rita's greatness was in her plays. She affected many lives with these productions. She is a single woman. She doesn't go home to someone who is there to lift her up. It is her and her alone when she goes home into her private moments. I believe in T.E.A.M. (Together Everyone Achieves More). We all need to be lifted up. We are not in this world alone. He lifted her up with his words. What if Albert wasn't there to support her? Would she have quit? She didn't, and many of her students went on to get performing arts scholarships. They have gone on to lead productive lives and raise a family. Why? Because someone cared.

Albert decided to try marriage once again. The woman had two children of her own. They had a biological father alive and who was involved in their lives to a certain extent. Jennifer, the youngest of the children, decided to join the Brownies (Girl Scouts). At this point in time, Dad had not yet married their mother and was probably in that place of questioning if he really ever wanted to marry again. Jennifer was very excited about getting to go to the dance with her daddy. The time came and he didn't come. She was left standing at the altar. This could have greatly affected her life. She could have lost all trust in men; maybe she would have questioned if there was any man that loved her. Albert stepped in without missing a beat and took Jennifer to the father-daughter dance. He didn't have to. It wasn't his daughter. Out of his love, he let this 5-year-old girl know that she was loved. More greatly, he let her know that men will love you and you are worthy of love.

Dad became her father. He adopted her and she became his daughter. As an adult, Jennifer has been able to get married and most importantly stay married. She married young and is still married to this day. She told me this is the story she remembers most about Albert.

Love does conquer all.

I know why we fought like we did. Dad wasn't becoming his best in my teen years. I wanted my father. He was accepting less than perfect for himself. HE was the one whining and complaining that is was becoming too hard. I fought with him because he was still my father, the father who stopped and told me, "Son, don't you ever give up. I don't care how bad it hurts, no matter how bad the pain gets, DON'T YOU EVER GIVE UP." It was us keeping each other sharp. It was his truth looking back into his own eyes and telling him to remember this side of himself once again. He instilled it into me and now I was putting it back onto him.

I was told a few times by his new wife that Albert was talking about killing himself. I never believed her. I shook it off when she would tell me. Why? Because this is the same man who told me to never give up despite "how bad the pain got" (his words coming back on him). I knew he wouldn't either.

There are some people who are just not good for one another. The relationship between my father and his second wife was a tornado meeting a volcano. It was volatile, and I am not sure if either one of them benefitted from each other. Their deficiencies drove them to each other. In writing my book and reflecting on my life, I have learned that this is not love, but is more of a sickness.

I do have regrets. I regret not having the man that raised me from birth to 10 years old. I wanted him all of my life. Where did he go? I did get him back in the end. It took a bullet to the head for that man to return to us. WE did get to see his heart for his last season in life.

My father's journey is complete. Some believe there are signs to give us confirmation about things in our lives. My father called me on 7/07/07 to tell me he loved me. (The bookend conversation). He lay in his bed with a hole in his skull not being able to move or articulate words for the most part of 7 years. In the Christian faith 3 represents the Trinity, 40 represents the test, and 7 is completion. My father's journey was completed.

Dad, thank you for taking the time to stop, to turn around and tell me to "never give up." Thank you for telling Rita, "You keep going, girl." Thank you for taking Jennifer to the father-daughter dance. You did make a difference in our lives.

My personal journey of the son did not end with the Eulogy of my father in May of 2014. I have continued to heal, to grow and to move forward. As the 400 meter hurdle of my life continues I press forward. I will run my race with everything I've got until it is finished. I hope you will do the same as you continue on your own journey, your own race in this life.

> *"...those who hope in the Lord will renew their strength. They will soar on wings like eagles; they will run and not grow weary, they will walk and not be faint."*
>
> Isaiah 40:31

Marcus Santi

SPECIAL THANKS:

These are the people who played major roles in my life:

Stephen Mansour – my tennis coach as a junior tennis player. You are still my friend today and I'm glad of it. Coming to see you once a week when I was in 7th - 8th grade made a big difference in my life.

Donna Spicer – I know you no longer go by Spicer but in my mind you will always be Mrs. Spicer. You were a mom to me when I really needed one.

Brandon Spicer – You are my best friend. You, just like your mother will always have a specific title: Best Friend

Kevin Argo – Another Best Friend. Too many stories to tell and I know you are hoping I DON'T tell any of them. LOL GO TIGERS

Tommy Bronson – you challenged me to fight you in 6th grade. I'll never forget that. I valued you as a great competitor. To steal a line from some receiver "That's my quarterback …that's my quarter back." One of the greatest achievements our group of friends has is winning the flag football league. None of us even had high school football experience and we beat teams with former college football athletes playing on them.

Robert and Barbara Santi – you provided refuge from my troubled home. You believed in me.

Mr. Hill – you spent your free time with me on the track to help me accomplish my goals.

Argo Family – Mr. and Mrs. Argo, thanks for opening your home to me which coincidently allowed me to literally finish high school.

Lesli Akers – There are people in this world who bring out the ultimate best in others. You're one of those. I'm lucky to know you.

About the Author

Marcus Santi is a coach, trainer and motivational speaker. He became a coach after his days as an elite track athlete. He now helps guide NFL, college, high school, and grade school athletes to achieve their own goals in and off the field. He still competes in Master's Track and Field annually at national competitions and has had the honor to represent America at the 2007 Master's World Championship of Track and Field held in Italy, where he anchored the 4x400 meter relay team to a silver medal. For the past two years he has ranked top 5 in the world in his age group for the 400m hurdles. Marcus continues to passionately love sports. It is something he and his father shared. He embraced T.E.A.M. (Together Everyone Achieves More) because of sports, especially by way of coaching.

www.ingramcontent.com/pod-product-compliance
Lightning Source LLC
LaVergne TN
LVHW051556070426
835507LV00021B/2611